Foreword by a Player

I remember being on the range at Quinta da Marinha before the 2004 Portuguese Open – I was hitting the ball all over the place. It was shocking. Nothing seemed to work. Looking back, I can still see the other players on the range, watching me moan and curse. I just couldn't hit the ball. I telephoned Dr. John Pates on my mobile and we arranged to meet the very next day before I teed off in the tournament.

We worked together for a couple of hours-not on my swing or anything technical, just on trying to relax and letting it happen. The rest is history as I went on to win my first tournament since 1995.

Without Dr. John I would have missed the cut in Portugal. There is no question about that. That's how badly I was playing and how good Dr. John is. Dr. John is the best Psychologist I have ever worked with, no question. He has made a huge difference to the way I play golf. Dr. John Turned me into a champion again.

I have worked with one or two sports psychologists in my time as a professional. Dr. John is the best by a long way. Before I met him, my biggest concern on a golf course was that under pressure, I had nothing to fall back on. If my game wasn't up to scratch, I knew when the pressure came it was all over – end of story. I'd blow the tournament.

I needed to find a way to think on the course to stop that. Dr. John taught me how.

A lot of the time I was seeing guys who would tell me about my subconscious mind – it's there but you are not aware of it, they said. Well, that didn't help me at all. I needed something I could actually think of during a round, something concrete that I could put into practice. Dr. John taught me how to do that.

I fractured my hand really badly in 2000 and I was out of the game for 15 months. Then when I came back I struggled for two years to regain any kind of form. The magic was just gone. I tried everything but couldn't get it back. I managed to get my card at the tour school and then I met Dr. John in April 2003.

My game really took off almost from the day began working together. I managed to keep my card in 2003 without much trouble – the following year I played great and finished in the top 40 of the order of merit and then in 2005 I won my first tournament since 1995. In 2006 I successfully defended the Portuguese open title and finished in the top 50 in the world. I owe so much to him. Dr. John has helped my whole game.

I will give you an interesting statistic that will show the change. In 2003 I was 110th in the putting statistics on the tour – I had really struggled on the greens. Then with Dr. John's help and unique putting methods the following year I came 5th. I am now ranked the 3rd best putter on the tour. With Dr. John's help I have gone from 30 putts per round to 28 which is six shots a tournament and that's a huge difference.

Dr. John taught me if I focus on the front part of the ball and hit through that point it would stop me from thinking about technique and improve my ball strike.

In the early part of my career I was a good putter, then I lost it. I don't know why. I just couldn't get the ball in the hole. I suppose I got wrapped up in the technique too much. He has given me very simple thoughts and they work. You'll learn about them in this book.

If you want to improve your golf, you must work on your mental game as well as your swing. I admit you need good technique to shoot low but the great thing about golf is that we all have our own targets. On the Tour we want to win tournaments whereas the club golfer wants to win the club medal and get his handicap down. The pressures are still the same.

I bet you know players at your club who knock the ball around nicely with their friends but when you put a card in their hand everything changes. They freeze and go to pieces. They can only play well when it doesn't matter.

In this book Dr. John will teach you the same techniques he uses with me and all the other Tour players he has helped. They are not complicated or difficult to understand. Dr. John Knows all the science behind his teaching but you wont be aware of that. He filters through the science using simple language that anyone can understand. It's not mumbo jumbo and jargon.

Dr. John taught me how to become a champion again. The secret is revealed in the pages of this book. Follow his teaching and you'll have a much better chance of fulfilling your golf dreams, whether your handicap is 28 or scratch.

Enter the Zone

(How to think and play like a champion)

by

Dr. John Pates
Dean Robertson
Mike Gardner

Grosvenor House
Publishing Limited

This book is published by
Grosvenor House Publishing Ltd
28-30 High Street, Guildford, Surrey, GU1 3HY.
www.grosvenorhousepublishing.co.uk

A CIP record for this book
is available from the British Library

ISBN 978-1-906645-32-8

Cover photograph: Dean Robertson tees off on the
18th hole of the Old Course at St Andrews

Contents

Dean Robertson's
Journey into the Zone

The date is May 18, 1998. The time: around 4pm. Former Walker Cup player Dean Robertson is on the 14th tee at Wentworth in the final round of the Volvo PGA Championships. The pressure is weighing down on him in great waves but even though the situation is unfamiliar to him, Dean is 'in the zone', a state he does not know much about apart from the certain knowledge that, whatever it is, he is experiencing an incredible sensation, now, when he needs it most.

There are just five holes remaining and Dean is holding a one-shot lead in the biggest tournament of his life. He is playing in the final two-ball and has just birdied the 13th to take him to five-under-par for the round. Every shot he has hit today has been perfect - drives, irons, putts – every one. Dean has the sense that he is a computer programme, and it is scientifically impossible for him to deviate from the perfect swing plane, each shot arrowing towards the target, drawn in by an invisible and irresistible force. So far his performance has been simple and uncomplicated; excellence is coming naturally, a part of his vital energy. And even the presence of the BBC cameras and tens of thousands of spectators do not unsettle him.

The enormity of the occasion would normally introduce self-doubt that might cripple his ability to perform, nerves might spread though his body like theoretical blocks of cement around his feet. But not now. And there's more.

Dean is playing with Colin Montgomerie, the world number three and one of the greatest players in British golfing history. Monty, who has won the European Order of Merit for the previous six years, is playing superbly, and the disparity in the credentials of the two players is extreme. Tournament wins: Monty 19, Dean 0. Earnings: Monty £4.8m, Dean £337,000. European ranking: Monty 1, Dean 73. This confrontation today, theoretically at least, is imbalanced, the golfing equivalent of a supermarket trolley meeting an articulated truck. But this evidence has not occurred to Dean. And even if it had, he would have paid no attention to it - he *knows* he is going to win. Confidence glows in him. He is invincible.

Dean is 'in the zone' and playing the best golf of his life, and though he does not know how he got here, he is enjoying the moment, failure not entering his mind, not for a moment, just the next shot, each one a gentle step on an inevitable journey towards the title.

Then it all goes wrong. He crashes out of the zone and is transported back to the present, among the crowds, and the cameras, the pressure, and the fear of failure, self-doubt gnawing away at his insides. The change is inexplicable and instant, as if someone had turned off an electric switch. His performance changes from magnificent to mediocre and the tournament and £200,000 slips through his fingers dramatically, watched by more than 10 million BBC viewers around the UK and across Europe. Here Dean tells the story in his own words.

∽

I'm a very excitable person on and off the golf course. I'm not scared to admit that I get nervous when I'm playing. My palms begin to sweat and my heart rate goes up. The biggest learning experience for me was in 1998 in the Volvo PGA. I was in the last group on the last day playing with Colin Montgomerie. I think I was four or five under for the round and I'd just birdied 13 and with five holes to play I was a shot in the lead.

Monty had pulled his tee shot long and left on the par three 14th and looked like making a bogey. I hit a nice five iron to the top tier but my ball came all the way back to the bottom. I hit a nice putt which finished about $2^1/_2$ feet short, up the hill with a slight curving right-to-left borrow. Monty made bogey and then, all of a sudden, everything started to go wrong.

I didn't know what 'the zone' was, not back then. But I knew I had been in control even though I was incredibly nervous. There were maybe 20,000 people around, all funnelling towards us at Wentworth but I had been oblivious to them, even all the cheering. I was in the zone but I didn't realise how or why. I just knew everything was going smoothly.

Then, for some reason, I started thinking about the outcome. I was over the putt and I said to myself: 'Let's just knock this in.' Then I thought: 'Oh my God. I've got this for a two-shot lead with four holes to go.' I almost wished the ball into the hole. So I wasn't thinking about the putt, I was thinking about other things which diminished my concentration.

My muscles had become tight and I under-hit the putt. It took more break and missed on the left side. I tapped in the next one and I had four holes to go with a one-shot lead.

This was the PGA Championship, our flagship event on the European Tour. It was the first time I had been in contention for a major event and I remember walking off the green and feeling horrific. From not being aware of a single person, I could see everybody. On the 15th tee I was out of control. I'd lost my rhythm and my focus and from being channelled and thinking about positioning shots on certain parts of the fairway and green, I was thinking about just getting the ball anywhere between the trees. I wanted to make contact and I was wishing the ball down the fairway. All I could think of was millions of people watching on TV.

I managed to make contact down the left and then somehow hit a four-iron onto the green and two-putted. But Monty made an unbelievable birdie, holing a long swinging putt and upping the pressure. So, all of a sudden, we were level with three to go.

On 16 I had hit three-wood off the tee every day and always on the right side of the fairway. It was a shot that had not troubled me before. But this time I did not compose myself. I was still running away too quickly internally. My heart-rate was going way too fast and my mind wasn't focused. I felt like a boxer getting punched in the stomach.

I didn't have a clue what to do. I began thinking about the enormity of winning the tournament, all the outcomes - the 10-year exemption, more than £200,000 prize money, playing with Colin Montgomerie in our biggest tournament.

And here I was, just a wee golfer from Paisley. I would never have thought in my wildest dreams that I would be here, in this situation. On the tee I was just going through the motions and I turned my three-wood left, over the trap, beyond a ditch and into some rhododendron bushes. I made double bogey, so now I'm two shots behind.

I'm totally shell-shocked and saying to myself: 'What are you doing? You've blown it.' Somehow I managed a par on 17 and on 18 I still couldn't compose myself, though I managed a birdie with a good putt which made me feel better. I finished two shots behind Monty and totally drained. It was a learning experience but I have to say I was happy to be out of there.

Dean's final round of 70, two-under-par, had earned him a share of fifth place alongside Matt Hallberg, Thomas Bjorn, Peter Lonard and Andrew Coltart. He picked up a cheque for £37,000, which, on the face of it, if you are a bus driver or a plumber or a postman, might not seem too bad a return for four days' work. But Dean's experience had troubled him. One shot less and he could have earned £89,000, two less and he might have been the champion, holding the trophy, the exemption, the Major invitations and £200,000. He'd been so near. And Dean was convinced his failure was mental, that he had lost concentration when he needed it most. His fall from the zone was sudden and inexplicable. When he was an amateur, Dean had earned a reputation for getting the job done. His titles had been achieved using something sportsmen refer to as 'bottle', which is more appropriate for explosive games such as soccer, rugby or boxing, where the margin for failure is measured in feet rather than fractions of inches that separate golfing champions from also-rans. Now he was with the big boys, among the greatest players in the world, and such a simplistic view on his mental game was not enough. Never would be.

That season spluttered along, confirming his frustrating reputation for unfulfilled potential. His golf was plagued by extremes and inconsistency - short-term, wonderful golf followed by nagging failures.

Dean went on to finish 67th in the German Open, followed by 36th (English Open), 46th (French Open), 53rd (Irish Open) and 13th at Loch Lomond. He was making money and he knew that low rounds were more likely to be accomplished when he was in the zone. What Dean did not know was how to get there, how to tap in to the mental calm that occasionally touched him, a euphoric frame of mind that randomly blessed him without warning, a gift from heaven, falling out of the sky. Then it would disappear, taken from him by unknown forces. Sometimes he felt it was so close he could reach out and touch it. Then it would fade away.

In 1999, Dean missed the cut in the Portuguese Open after mediocre rounds of 77 and 82. The following week he came 33rd in the Spanish Open, before heading for Italy, praying for a visit from the 'zone' gods. They came. And they stayed. And he won.

⌒

I was a shot behind Padraig Harrington with one round to play. We were last out in the final round and I played fantastic. I was in my zone big-time and I had made a host of birdies. I stood on the tee at the par three 16th and

I had a one-shot lead. I was so pumped up that I thought it was a four-iron but I decided to hit a five hard. I could feel myself running into the old Wentworth thing but I managed to focus on the target, simple stuff like that.

I didn't really know what I was doing. I suppose I was just playing the game I loved without analysing it. Well, I went into a bunker where I had a terrible, plugged lie but I hit an unbelievable shot to four feet and holed it for three. Over the putt I felt great, not like Wentworth, just calm and composed, and, as I've already said, I don't know why. Then, all of a sudden, it happened again on the 17th tee, just like at Wentworth. I can't explain it.

My practice swing felt great. I picked my spot and just before I hit the ball I asked myself: 'Now where am I hitting this?' Well, I hit a big block 70 yards to the right. In fact, it was so far off-line it was OK. I got away with it but there was a panic going through my body. I had a two-shot lead with two holes to go. I kept thinking: 'let's bring this thing in,' like I was hooking a big fish.

Of course, the worst thing you can ever think of in the world is outcome. Just for a split-second I let myself get ahead. 'Just two holes to go. This is brilliant. I've got a bit of a buffer.' But you can't relax thinking like that. Somehow I managed to get tuned in again and focused and I hit a seven iron on to the front of the green. Padraig three-putted, so I had got out of jail and again I started thinking that if I holed my second putt I'd have three shots to spare. How good is that? I could really savour the moment and enjoy going up the last. So what happened? I missed it.

'Oh no. Nightmare,' I thought. I was up and down like a yo-yo but I refocused again and made a good drive. Padraig hit a great second to ten feet. At that point there was so much adrenalin I could hit any club any distance. My caddie gave me a wedge, though we had 148 yards to go. I pulled it slightly and it pitched in the middle of the green but spun back to the front, leaving me a 40-foot putt across a big slope.

Again I refocused and hit a great putt two-feet below the hole. Padraig holed his putt, which I knew he would. The crowd went mental but it didn't even register with me. I just walked over, went through my routine and knocked it in. I had stayed in my bubble and I won by one shot.

I had arrived and fulfilled my dream. But where did I go from here? I started thinking about stuff like Ryder Cups, winning more tournaments and playing in the Majors. At that time, players were starting to talk about goals. I didn't know what goals were. For me they had become walls I was building to climb over. Then I met Dr. John Pates and he's helping me knock these walls down, brick by brick.

Before Dean met sports psychologist Dr. John Pates and began using mental techniques, his inconsistency had been spectacular. He was beginning to become discouraged by the massive disparity of performance which had troubled him for several seasons. The week after he had played the best golf of his life in Italy, winning £100,000 for his incredible 17-under-par total, Dean missed the cut in the French Open, finishing 148th after an opening round of 79. His variations were that extreme, champion to hacker in seven days.

He bounced back two weeks later to make the top ten in the English Open, earning £15,000 at 12 under. Seven days later he was left shaking his head in Ireland after another missed cut and a tie for 126th.

Dean's most emphatic example of inconsistency came at Gleneagles in the Scottish PGA Championships. He opened with an 83, which is an incredibly high total, the golfing equivalent of, say, a Premiership striker missing 10 penalties on the row. The following day Dean shot a four-under 68, which was an improvement of 15 shots, an unlikely accomplishment comparable with Cilla Black knocking out Mike Tyson.

Dean headed for Madrid, still searching for an answer. That was when he met Dr. John Pates and his life changed for ever.

~

In the mid-90s, there were no Tour players talking to golf psychologists. If you did, there was something wrong with you. Yet even when I was playing at my optimum level I was still making mental errors. Probably everyone else was, too, so I was still able to finish with some top performances.

Then, some of the top players realised that the mental side could help them reduce mistakes. I have always been a great one for thinking outcomes. And now, using Dr. John Pates's teaching, I understand what happens and why that is such a bad thing. You just can't play well doing that. It is impossible. Dr. John taught me about the process, about concepts such as 'left brain and right brain' - things I knew nothing about.

What I did know, whether I was playing at Wentworth, in the final round of the Italian Open or in any tournament, was that I always had swing thoughts on the course. I needed them and I was very analytical.

I would be over a shot and at certain times I had three swing thoughts. As I waggled the club, I would be saying to myself: 'Keep your left knee in, rotate and stay tall.' This was how I played all the time and it was killing me, though I didn't know that at the time. I think my swing thought at Wentworth was 'quiet the legs and tall,' if I remember correctly.

I had seen Dr. John around the Tour. I thought this big guy was a fitness instructor. Seeing him about, he was a daunting figure. Dr. John is 6ft 5ins tall and very athletic-looking with a stride that makes him look like a triple-jumper.

I was playing with Gary Emerson in Madrid and I started with five birdies in the first six holes. Dr. John was walking around with Gary and all of a sudden, for no reason I could think of, I just frittered away all those shots. That kind of thing was happening to me all the time. I came off the course and I was gobsmacked and devastated. I thought: 'This bloody game is doing my head in.' There was no logic to explain what had happened. After I had finished, I met Dr. John.

'How are you doing, big man?' I asked him. 'Did you watch that out there today? What did you think?'

'Incredible,' he answered.

'How come I go to pot all the time?' I asked him.

We sat down together and he explained his basic philosophy. I understood him but I wanted to know why, all my life, I had had so much trouble applying it.

'I thought you were going for a course record today,' Dr. John said.

'Aye, so did I but I got too excited and I just crashed,' I told him.

I knew I had to be relaxed to play well and that sometimes I got too excited and as a result, lost control of my emotions.

I remember saying to Dr. John: 'Tell me your deal. Are you just another one of these bullshit guys? I am a sceptic. What have you got?'

I've been playing golf for 25 years and I knew the mind is very important, but I still couldn't master it. So we went to the range there and then. Before we began hitting any balls, I told Dr. John I felt relaxed but it wasn't how I performed here, on the range, that was the problem. It was out on the course, where it mattered.

In time, Dr. John taught me to develop my pre-shot routine to include relaxation. On the first tee of a tournament, I take my club out of the bag and begin to relax physically. I put my hands on the club and squeeze my elbows into my stomach, progressively, slowly increasing the tension from a count of one to five. No one around me knows what I am doing. Then I relax and start mental relaxation by taking myself away in my mind from the situation.

For example, if I was back on the 16th tee at Wentworth, using these techniques I could have handled the pressure much better. In my mind I would have taken myself to an environment I felt comfortable in. It might have been my favourite beach, for example. That would have changed how I felt, which in, turn changes the way I play.

Your mind can take you anywhere you want. So I can walk into my home and the tension goes. It's easier if your eyes are closed and you can get away with it if you wear sunglasses. It shouldn't matter but I am conscious of people staring, wondering what I am doing.

The place you go to in your mind is up to you. Dr. John's favourite place is Loch Lomond. As for me, well, I have different places for different situations. If the weather is cold, I imagine I am soaking in a hot bath and if it is really warm, say I'm playing in Australia or Malaysia, I imagine I'm in a cool swimming pool. You can really access these feelings. It only takes a few seconds but it takes your mind away from where you are and quietens down your body. Talking about it makes the process seem long but it only takes between five and ten seconds.

So I'm in this swimming pool and seeing myself soaking in the cool water. Another trick we use is imagining the water going flat-calm and that's what we call a 'mantra'. This has a real calming effect, so if you are at Loch Lomond looking across the water you see all the ripples and the wind. Then, in your mind, you make it calm and still and that imagery brings your heart beat and blood pressure down. That takes you to a level you can operate from. I wish I'd had this knowledge at Wentworth.

Some thoughts might give you better clarity than others. It's all about finding out what works for you. If you were playing in St Andrews in October, wrapped up with your mitts on, you wouldn't want to imagine you are in a cold swimming pool. That would be the last place you would want to go. But a hot bath, well, that would be likely to help you.

From there I go on a journey. I picture myself going up to the target, going to the green and maybe holding the pin, feeling the weight of it. Then I'll come back to myself and see myself standing on the fairway or on the tee. Jack Nicklaus called it going to the movies. Nick Price talks about his third eye. I might change the colour of the flag from yellow to red, it's all about putting images into your mind that will block out thoughts of bunkers, money, spectators or trees, stuff like that - outcomes.

We call this imagery. So after I feel calm I might see myself playing the perfect shot, from a certain angle. Then I would walk into myself, my perfect self and sense the feeling of the shot. I might be looking at myself in a giant cinema screen, but the image is always the same: the perfect shot. These thoughts can help you do whatever you want if the image is clear enough.

The last thing I do is go back on a quick journey to the pin. Then I drop the image and think target. So I've programmed myself, imagined where I want to go in my mind and I'm ready to go. I don't see the ball, just the target. It really works.

If, for example, I am struggling to calm myself, if I am really nervous and being bombarded with all these external factors, Dr. John has taught me to use what he calls external imagery.

You imagine you have just had a satisfactory video lesson and you are watching yourself on a television screen. You can use different camera angles, too, perhaps from above or behind. One thing is constant: every time you hit a shot it's perfect, whatever club you are using the shot is the best you have ever hit in your life. You are emotionally detaching yourself from the situation so that if you're really excited, these thoughts help to produce that calming feeling you are looking for.

Personally, I don't have a key for taking the club back but if you need one you might want to think of the target, keep it in your mind and imagine you are a video recorder and you are pressing the play button. And, of course, the video will be of your perfect swing.

All these concepts are difficult to explain. I'm still learning what the best way is for me. There are lots of different variations and they all work, but some work better than others. You have to find out what suits you.

You have to try to detach yourself from the situation completely. People who can walk across hot coals in their bare feet use the same principles. How can they do that? They do it by controlling their minds. Golfers need to learn how to do that by using imagery to change their state of mind. Take yourself on a journey to your favourite places.

We daydream all the time. Dr. John's philosophy is completely new. There is definitely no one who has tapped into his ideas. I'll give you an example of how these techniques helped me overcome one of the toughest holes I have come across anywhere in the world.

In the Masters at Singapore this year I finished in the top ten. There was a brute of a hole on the course, a 220-yard par three all over water to an island green. There's a slight bale out to the left but the rough is long and there's a deep gulley. You can make any number from there.

It was the last round and the pressure was on. Everybody was hitting so far left, playing safe and running up some ridiculous numbers. It was a three-iron for me and I remember being very nervous. It's a hole that gets the heart-rate up; the degree of difficulty is so high.

In the final round I knew if I held things together I was in for a good finish. On the 16th tee I combined relaxation techniques, both physical and mental. The wind was off the left so I selected my target, the left edge of the green and went on a journey accessing the perfect image of myself. Then I went back to the target and in my mind I imagined the blue water turning green. The water became grass and all I could see was the pin and a beautiful fairway. That way I blanked everything out but the target. Your imagination is very powerful. I hit a three-iron straight on the line I had chosen, exactly as I had imagined to within 10 feet. It was one of the finest shots I had ever hit and I went on to hole the birdie putt. I think I was two-under on that hole all week.

Before meeting Dr. John I would have approached the hole differently. I would have aimed down the left and hoped for the best. I would have been thinking, 'please go on the green, and don't leak it right.' Of course, as soon as you think that, you get what you pay attention to. That's how your mind works. If the last thing you think to yourself is, don't go in the water, you probably will. So whether you think of trees, lakes, bunkers or out of bounds, that's where you'll probably end up.

If you use Dr. John's teaching, you can stop yourself from doing that. Your mind can take you anywhere and these journeys can enable you to virtually do anything you want. Basically, it's about being creative.

Try it. Dr. John's teaching works for me and it can work for you, too.

CHAPTER ONE

How to Control your Nerves

Dean Robertson

I'm a confident person. You need confidence to play on
the Tour. But like all golfers nerves can affect the way I
play. I've never felt more nervous than I did in the Walker
Cup at Interlachen Country Club in Minnesota back in
1993. I was just 22 and we had a really young team
which included Padraig Harrington, Bradley Dredge,
Raymond Burns, Ian Pyman and my Scottish team-mate
Raymond Russell.

So we go over there and see all these stars, awesome
players such as Justin Leonard, Jay Sigel, Alan Doyle and
Tim Herron. Everyone said we were going to get
hammered and that's exactly what happened. I did OK
but it could have been so much better. The trouble was,
back then, I didn't know how to control my nerves.

My coach at the time was Bob Torrance. Of course,
ten years ago, psychology didn't exist. If you needed
a psychologist there was something wrong with you.
I didn't know a single player who used one, in fact, we
would have considered the need for a psychologist as a
weakness, not a strength.

To us, you had to have what everyone referred to as 'bottle' and a big heart. It was all about grinding and never giving in. That was about as far as the mental game went. If you had asked me then to talk about the mental side of golf I would have struggled to write down a couple of sentences.

Building up to the event, my game was spot on in every aspect. Even now, after all these years, I can still remember something my pal Raymond Russell said to me after a practice round. He said I was 'hotter than the weather,' which was boiling at the beginning of the week.

I was feeling what I call now 'excited nervous' which is not a bad thing. The course was tree-lined and very tough and there were thousands of spectators. The greens were really slick and none of the Great Britain and Ireland players could figure them out.

So I was feeling good about everything but the night before the first matches I couldn't sleep or eat. And I was off to the toilet every five minutes.

During the night there was a huge thunderstorm that lasted for ages and flooded the course. There was water everywhere. Looking back I can still see the fire engines trying to pump water off the course and out of the bunkers, which were like small swimming pools. The morning foursomes were cancelled and we had to wait in the locker room for hours before we found out that the singles were to be played in the afternoon.

I was to play Jay Sigel, who went on to win more points than anyone in Walker Cup history and clean up a fortune in the US Seniors. At that time I think I weighed about nine stone and Jay was this giant of a man. I shook hands with him on the first tee and thought to myself: 'How can I beat this guy?'

I looked around at the packed stands and the television cameras and realised we were on network TV in the States and the matches would be screened across Europe so there would be millions of people watching us. I'd been under pressure before but I had never experienced anything like this.

Somehow I won 3 and 2 through steady, controlled play. I managed to get the job done. Jay made the odd mistake while I played controlled golf. Given the circumstances I thought I played fantastic. So despite the nerves, I was confident and successfully handled my nerves but I had no idea how or on any given day if I would be successful. I suppose it was luck and a touch of that magical gift called 'bottle.' I thought I had my fair share but then I found out the next day how quickly it can all go wrong if you don't know how your mind works.

I played with Raymond against Tim Herron and Dr. John Harris and we lost by one hole. The sparkle had just gone. The team was getting hammered and the pressure built up on all of us.

I walked off the 18th tee emotionally drained but I was told I was due on the first tee immediately. I was leading off the afternoon singles so someone stuck a sandwich in my hand and said: 'Eat that while you're playing.'

Not surprisingly I lost 4 and 3 to Allan Doyle, which was naturally disappointing. The point of the story is that I was nervous big-time in the morning but I had managed to control my feelings to play pretty good golf. I didn't know how, not then. It just kind of happened and I was grateful for it. But in the afternoon, and the next day, my nerves got the better of me and I just couldn't come up with a solution.

Just a couple of months before I played in the Walker Cup I was defending the Scottish Amateur Strokeplay championship at St Andrews on the Jubilee and New Course.

I had won so many amateur events that year that I felt I was the king of the castle in Scotland. It was as if I was bulletproof and playing well had become a habit. But as soon as you lose track of your game-plan things can go wrong. Within a few minutes or even between shots you can lose confidence and begin to get nervous and you're left with a lost tournament in less time than it takes to clap your hands. There's no warning. It just happens. One minute everything is perfect and the next you've missed a short putt or carved a vital tee shot out-of-bounds. That's what happened to me at St Andrew's.

I was in the penultimate group and I had moved through the field perfectly. My golf had been excellent all week and I stepped onto the last tee in the last round with a one-shot lead. All I needed was a par to win and even a bogey might have been good enough.

Then it happened. I had been in control for four days, for the best part of 20 hours, but now, when all I had to do was hit the fairway, my mind was starting to race away with thoughts about what it would mean to me to win the championship again, especially here at St Andrews. The nerves just crashed around me like a great black cloud. There was so much emotion inside me, I didn't know what to do. The best word I can use to describe how I was feeling is 'wobbly.' Most golfers will understand that.

I still laugh when I look back at that tee shot now. I managed to block my driver at least 50 yards right, straight into the greenkeepers' compound and out of bounds. I went on to make a double bogey and lost the tournament by a shot. It was a terrible feeling that I had no explanation for.

So the point of these two stories is that controlling nerves is something we all need to do to play our best. It doesn't have to be random or lucky, like it was for me in the Walker Cup. You can learn how to control nerves using scientific techniques, the same techniques all the top Tour players use now, including Tiger Woods, Davis Love III and Darren Clarke.

The problems are exactly the same for a seasoned tournament professional as they are for a county player making his debut or someone trying to get his handicap cut in the monthly medal. Our minds all work the same way.

Dr. John Pates has given me the knowledge to cope with my nerves most of the time. Now, I'm pretty sure if I could go back to St Andrews, on the 18th tee on the Jubilee course in the last round of the Scottish Strokeplay championships, I would get the job done. I'm confident I could have hit that fairway and made the par I needed.

This is how I might have done it.

There are many techniques and this book will teach them to you though you'll have to experiment and discover what works for you. So back to St Andrews.

Firstly I would have conducted what we call 'progressive relaxation.' That means squeezing the grip of the club tightly, increasing the tension in my hands and through my arms and along to my chest and shoulder blades. After a few seconds I would just let go and the tension would be released. It's amazing. Anxiety just fizzes away like you've just opened a bottle of Coca Cola.

But the most important thing is mental relaxation. The situation is making me overexcited so I would take a mental journey away from there, away from the crowds and the tight fairway and the pressure. Your mind can take you anywhere you want. You could be back home soaking in a hot bath or you might want to imagine you are relaxing by a swimming pool at your favourite holiday resort. It only takes a few seconds but that will break the pattern that is creating the tension.

I sometimes picture myself paddling on the shores of Loch Lomond, which is one of my favourite places and somewhere that makes me feel relaxed and comfortable, exactly the feelings I want to experience now.

The more real you make your imaginary journey, the more the image will help you. Make the colours bright, hear the sounds, and use your imagination to help you. You can call on different images for different situations. If it's bitterly cold I'll want to travel to somewhere hot, say to a beach in the Caribbean, and I'll imagine the sand between my toes and the sun burning from the blue sky, and I'll be relaxing and listening to my favourite music without a care in the world. I'll hear the birds and the ocean as the images cascade over me.

This will completely break the programme of thinking of the shot, or the importance of the situation, or the pressure or how much it would mean if I could pull off just one more good shot. Believe me, professionals think exactly the way amateurs do.

An amateur will be just as nervous playing in his weekend medal or trying to win an area title as unknown American Ben Curtis was winning the Open at Royal St George's in 2003. It's all relative to the level you're competing at.

So I'm almost ready to play the big shot now. But there are still a couple of techniques that I can call on if I need to. I can relive how I felt when I played my best round of golf or my best tee shot in similar circumstances. This will be a pleasant sensation that will make me smile and calm and relax me. Make your journey real and draw on its power. Then I might want to control my breathing.

When you're nervous your breathing gets quick and short and it's important to take a few, long, deep breaths in through your nose and exhaling through your mouth. Nobody needs to see you do this or squeeze the club or concentrate. The whole thing only takes a few seconds but it will have a dramatic impact on your ability to play the important shot

Finally there's the pre-shot routine. This is physical and it is mental and we'll be going into this in detail in a subsequent chapter.

So now I'm ready to play the pressure shot. Only this time I'm feeling good and confident and there will be no groans from the crowd, no wild blocks out of bounds. This time my mind is strong and the ball's away, 280 yards down the fairway with a touch of draw into the perfect position, just a wedge from the green and the championship that means so much to me.

How to Control your Nerves

Dr. John Pates

Everyone gets nervous on the golf course. Even Tiger Woods. One of the reasons he is such a great champion is because he knows how to deal with nerves when the heat is on. You will feel the same emotions in a club competition as Tiger does on the back nine of a Major championship. Our minds work the same way.

You might get anxious on the first tee, in bunkers, hitting over water or if you need to par the 18th to win the monthly medal or reduce your handicap. I'm going to teach you how to control your nerves by telling you a story about a European Tour player who was so nervous he could barely speak.

We're going back to the 2002 Italian Open at Rome's Olgiata Golf Club. I had been working with Gary Emerson for a few weeks and he had been making steady progress after a slow start to the season. He was plagued by inconsistency in the early part of the year, missing 11 cuts in his first 20 tournaments and making just £44,000. Then he started to play better, making nine cuts from the last 11 events and winning more than £70,000. Now he was within a whisker of getting in the top 115 of the Order of Merit and earning his card for another year. But he still needed a decent finish in the final event of the season in Italy or other players would take his place.

So you can imagine the pressure he was under. Two average rounds and he's off the Tour with an uncertain future and no income. Gary had been unlucky in Madrid the week before when he had missed the cut in the Spanish Open after struggling to recover from flu. He needed to win around £3,500 to keep his card so now, in Italy, he only had one chance, and as you probably know, you don't get a penny if you miss the cut. His closest rivals were Phil Golding and Gordon Brand Jnr, who had both accumulated more money than Gary at the start of the Italian Open.

He telephoned me and explained how important Italy was to him and that he needed my help. I had been delayed travelling from Madrid so I couldn't meet Gary until he had completed his first round. There was bad news waiting for me. Gary had shot a two-over-par 74.

We examined his round and, despite his disappointment, Gary was pleased that he had finished strongly following a dreadful start. He was dead and buried after four holes at five-over-par and pretty much last in the whole tournament. But he dug deep and stuck to his routine, clawing back his round by shooting two-under for the last 13 holes. The mediocre score was largely down to inaccuracy off the tee – Gary hit just three fairways, and only 11 greens. He finished the day in 95th position, with just 15 players behind him, and 13 shots behind the leader - Ian Poulter, who had shot an incredible 61.

Gary had recovered from worse opening rounds than 74 before. He was a tough character. Experience teaches professional golfers to be patient. But Gary had no time.

He reckoned he needed a 67 just to make the cut in the second round.

To make matters worse, Gary's two primary opponents had produced remarkable scores, given the circumstances. Gordon Brand Jnr shot a four-under 68 to put him well up on the leaderboard in the top 15 and Philip Golding shot 66, the six-under total propelling him into the top four.

Then it started raining. And it didn't stop. Thunderstorms rocked the course and forced the postponement of the second round and the tournament was reduced to 54 holes.

I had arranged to meet Gary on the range on Saturday morning about an hour before he was due to tee off in the most important tournament of his life. I could see Gary hitting balls as I walked towards the range and it was obvious he was having problems. Even from a distance, his body language was bad and when I got closer I could see why. He was hitting his shots all over the place and the tension was there, on his face. Fifty minutes to go and he's swinging like a hacker. I'm pretty sure he even topped a couple of shots which is pretty rare for a Tour player.

"Don't worry Gary," I told him. "We'll get you sorted out in no time."

He nodded unconvincingly. The poor guy was so tense he could hardly speak and this was having a massive effect on him physically. Nerves had simply overwhelmed him to the point where he could barely swing the club. I sympathise with players in this situation. The pressure was extreme. His lifestyle and the welfare of his family were all going to be decided by how he hit a golf ball in less than hour. But I'm not here for sympathy. I'm here to help him and I knew we had to work out a way that would enable him to control his nerves and return to a mental state that would permit Gary to play good golf.

I explained to him that my guess was that the enormity of the situation had got to him. As I've already told you, we had worked together for a while so he knew my techniques and he had faith in them. The trouble was he needed a reminder.

I told Gary that we were going to work on three techniques to control his nerves and get him in the right frame of mind for the round. Firstly I wanted Gary to relax physically so we went through a routine that is familiar with all my Tour players. It's called progressive muscular relaxation. It works by increasing the tension in the parts of your body that tighten and debilitate your ability to play when nerves start getting the better of you. For Gary it is usually his hands and shoulders. Other players might feel more tense in their legs.

He stood back and held the club in front of him, concentrating on his hands, staring at them and thinking of nothing else. I started counting slowly, as we had done so many times before, and each time he increased the tension.

"One'" and Gary starts squeezing the club, gently applying pressure. "Two," and he squeezes tighter, "three," tighter, "four," tighter still and finally "five." Now Gary is squeezing the club so hard, his fingers have turned white and there's a grimace across his face. He holds the club for three or four seconds and then lets go. As he releases his grip, he stays focused on what happens in his fingers as the tension flows out of him as if by magic, the effect is immediate but it does not surprise me. I've seen it happen before, so many times.

Gary is already feeling better. But we still have a lot to do. He's nervous because he knows his tee time is imminent and his future is on the line. Gary now needs a mental routine to stop him focusing on the enormity of what is at stake. He has to create an internal environment that is comfortable to him. Then he can start hitting the ball properly. So the best thing he can do is leave here – get away from the range, the crowds, the tournament, the money and the pressure. He must switch off from the problems and escape into a comfortable environment. So he starts daydreaming, and goes on a mental journey to his favourite place. For Gary, it's easy - he's most comfortable at home, with his family, back at Dorset.

So Gary is closing his eyes now and he's gone, back to England in the time it takes to clap your hands. He's made this journey so many times that it's easy for him. Gary is parking his car, closing the door behind him, hearing the click as the door slams shut. It's a beautiful summer's day, and Gary looks up towards the deep blue sky, soaking in the sun. He's into his house now, placing his car keys on the table, as his wife Dawn kisses him on the cheek and tells him how much she has missed him.

Gary moves into the lounge, and a smile works across his face as his young daughters Georgina and Charlotte run to him, hugging him as he sits in his favourite seat with his favourite people in his favourite place. When you try this you must concentrate as strongly as possible to make your dream seem real. Imagine how comfortable the seat feels as you sit down; see the pictures on the wall, look at the ornaments on your mantelpiece and immerse yourself inside the image.

To complete Gary's picture, there's music playing too, the melody creating a perfect, relaxing backdrop to the powerful image he has created in his mind, sharing the most comfortable place in the world with the people who love him.

We're almost there now and there has been a dramatic change in his posture and expressions. He's happy and relaxed – Gary is in his mental bubble, which is keeping out negative thoughts like a force field. He does not know the science behind this. He doesn't have to. But a lot of physiological things are happening to him and they will contribute to his ability to play great golf under enormous pressure.

Gary's heart rate has slowed right down. His blood pressure has reduced significantly too. In modern slang, Gary has chilled out – he's cool.

"How are you feeling now?" I ask him.

"Much better," he answers. It has taken a while to explain to you in detail what we are doing but in reality, Gary has been concentrating for less than a minute. Yet the change has been remarkable.

Now he is almost ready to hit a ball. There is just one more technique that will help him. If I remember correctly, Gary had been using a seven iron. So now he takes his stance and follows his pre-shot routine, focusing on the flag in the distance. In his mind he records a moving image of the scene, as if he has a theoretical video camera inside his head. Psychologists call this 'taking a sub-modality of the image.' I remind him to focus on the colour of the flag fluttering 160 yards away. Back to the ball and that image of the flag is clear and powerful, his concentration is taken up with all that matters - the target. Gary is aware of the ball but it's not the ball that matters – it's the target

The ball's away now, high and straight, landing softly five or six feet to the right of the pin. Gary's delighted but we do not speak, as though he is fearful of breaking the magic. We go through the same routine again and again - two more seven irons and two more perfect shots, always the same pre-shot routine, aiming his body and his mind, the target etched in his subconscious. Physical relaxation, mental relaxation and target.

Gary changes his club a couple of times but the result is always the same - great shots, the strike perfect and effortless.

"That's enough," he says, thanking me, and he's away, a spring in his step as he walks purposefully towards the practice putting green.

I knew he was going to play well. And he did. Gary was three-under-par after 10 holes but when he bogeyed the 11th he needed to birdie two of the last seven holes to make the cut. He managed a four on the par five 15th, so you can imagine how he was feeling on the 18th tee, knowing he needed a birdie or his life on the Tour was over – at least for the following year. Unbelievably he made it to shoot an incredible 67, which was a formidable achievement given the circumstances.

I was waiting for Gary as he walked off the 18th green. I wanted to congratulate him on his remarkable accomplishment. He was ecstatic but it was too early for us to celebrate. He still had another mountain to climb in the final round. But at least he had given himself a chance.

Gary had clawed his way back into the tournament, making up four shots on Gordon Brand Jnr, who shot 71, and eight shots on Paul Golding, who had finished with a 75.

We talked briefly and Gary told me that he felt confident of pulling it off, however unlikely that might have seemed. He is a very competitive person, the kind of player who could dig deep. Gary had always fancied himself to come out on top in such adverse circumstances.

That 67 was a monumental feat, one of the finest accomplishments I had seen on the Tour, considering what was at stake, which was basically everything. He knew he wasn't going to get a second chance.

The next day we repeated the process just as we had the previous day - physical relaxation, mental relaxation and target. He squeezed his club tighter and tighter before letting go, visited his home and his family and focused on the target.

Gary played really well again. He was three-under for the round with five holes to go. Then he started looking at the leaderboards, which is something I can understand but try to discourage my players from doing. That can create a lot of a stress and make them outcome-orientated. There are exceptions to this rule. A minority of players play better when they are excited. They need to be on a high. Andrew Oldcorn is like that. So is Stephen Gallacher. But most players perform better when they are relaxed and comfortable.

The figures on the scoreboard gave him an idea of what he had to do. The numbers told him that Philip Golding was on his way to the round of his life – a faultless nine-under-par 63, including seven birdies and an eagle. And Gordon Brand Jnr was still two shots ahead of Gary. So although the exact score he had to shoot to keep his Tour card was too complicated to calculate with most of the field still out on the course, Gary knew he could not afford to drop any shots or he was out, back on the plane to England looking for a job.

He finished par, birdie, par, par, par before walking off the 18th green drained by the mental and physical pressure he had been under. He had shot 68 - four-under – to finish seven under for the tournament and comfortably in the top 50.

Gary headed for the airport with most of the field still out on the course and the mathematics of the situation so close and complicated, tournaments officials could not estimate his chances of keeping his card.

"It will be close, possibly down to one shot and a few pounds," he was told as he left the course. Gordon Brand Jnr went on to finish with a two-under 70 for a final total of seven-under and level with Gary in 44th position.

Philip's magnificent round could not save him but he came agonisingly close. For 30 minutes or so he occupied 13th position on his own but Englishman Andrew Marshall came in with a 68 to join Philip at 12-under for the tournament and take a few hundred pounds off his prize money.

Gary was landing at Heathrow airport when the final calculations had been made. He had earned just under £4,000, leaving him 116th on the Order of Merit, one position below automatic qualification but subsequent investigations revealed that Korean Charlie Wi was exempt, allowing Gary to move up one place and keep his card. He had finished just 70 euros ahead of Gordon Brand Jnr, who missed out on the European Tour in 2003 by the price of a box of golf balls.

Gary telephoned me from the airport. He was ecstatic and full of gratitude for my role in his wonderful performance. I was proud of him and pleased that the dramatic battle for the last available place on the Tour received comprehensive coverage in the media. Gary graciously gave me credit for my involvement and the subsequent publicity dramatically heightened my profile on the Tour and helped me pick up a host of other players the following season.

You can learn so much from Gary's experiences in Italy. Within five minutes he had been transformed from a nervous wreck who could hardly speak to a confident player who went on to play some of the best golf of his life under the most extreme pressure.

Summary

To control your nerves you must create a workable pre-shot routine. This will help you to relax which is the antidote to nerves, stress and anxiety. Start with a physical relaxation programme – remember, tighten your grip on the club progressively, counting to five and then letting go.

The hands are the most common place that will feel tense if you are nervous but it could be your legs or your arms. Find out where tension affects you and work on that area using the same principles as Gary did in Italy.

Then go on a mental journey, away from whatever it is that is making you nervous, to a place where you will feel relaxed. For most people this is usually at home with their families but it could be anywhere – for Dean it could be lying on a beach in the Caribbean. Finally focus on the target when you are actually hitting the ball.

The techniques that worked so dramatically to enable Gary to control his nerves and get in a mental state to play well in Italy can work for you too.

CHAPTER TWO

How to Develop Confidence

Dean Robertson

In 1999 I went to the first tournament of the year eager and full of expectation. I couldn't wait to get to the South Africa PGA Championships at Houghton Golf Club. I was convinced I was certain to put in a good perform-ance. I was practising really well on the range and every-thing was going great.

Yet I missed the cut after shooting 75 and 76 which wasn't too impressive. The following week at the South African Open at the Stellenbosch Golf Club it was the same story. I was playing great outside the tournament but ended up shooting 73 and 75 for yet another missed cut, each bad round denting my confidence, every bad shot chipping away in my mind.

I flew to Australia hoping my luck would change but it was just the same old story in the Heineken Classic at Perth - great on the range and in practice but a 73 and a 72 meant another cut missed. In practice I had all the confidence in the world but as soon as the tournament started I would play badly, in fact it was worse than that. I was diabolical. So in the tournament my confidence had gone completely and I didn't know where to look to get it back. What I knew with utter certainty was that without confidence I was facing a lot more missed cuts.

But my scores did not improve. The pattern continued in exactly the same way, no matter where I was - great in practice - useless in the tournament. My game was first-class but I just couldn't take it where it really mattered - into the tournament. My confidence was shattered.

I've looked back in the records and the early part of 1999 does not make good reading. I made just two cuts out of the first 10 tournaments, including a 78 in Malaysia, another 78 in the Portuguese Open and an awful 82 at Penha Longa in the Estoril Open. I had played 24 rounds and shot under par just five times. Then, right out of the blue, my game started to improve in the Spanish Open at Golf El Prat, just outside Barcelona.

I made the cut and though my scores were nothing spectacular that was a good feeling. At the weekend I started to come good. I played the last round with Gary Emerson and I managed a 67 when everything started falling into place. My putting had been suffering through a lack of confidence but I was beginning to putt well again. But nothing prepared me for what happened the following week - I won the Italian Open, probably my greatest golfing achievement. On top of that I earned over £120,000 which was five times more than I had won in the previous 11 tournaments.

My change of form was totally inexplicable. All the time I was playing badly I was working really hard and asking myself: 'How did I hit such an awful shot?' I was going over everything in my mind, convinced that the problem was something technically wrong with my swing. But when I went to Italy I was practising so well that I decided to draw on the memories of all the great shots I was hitting away from the tournament. That brought my confidence flooding back.

Rather than focusing on the good points I had been stuck in a rut, concentrating on what I didn't want to do. I now know that the quality of your shots reflect what you pay attention to. If the last thing you look at on the tee is a bunker, that's probably where you'll end up.

All the time I was missing cuts the technical fault I was working on was not losing my height. So during a tournament, I kept saying to myself: 'keep your height,' but it didn't do any good.

The best help I had was from my caddie, Brian Byrne. He never lost faith in me and kept on saying: 'Be patient. You never know what's around the corner.' That relaxed me. When you are a tournament player who is missing cuts you get more and more tense and nervous. I went to South Africa, Malaysia, Australia and back to Dubai and I didn't make a bean. I had spent around £15,000 and hadn't made a cent. I was surrounding myself with negativity and now I know the solution was there, right under my nose. The answer wasn't technical it was mental. I needed to get my confidence back quickly.

The whole cycle repeated itself early in 2003. The difference then was that with Dr. John Pates' help I knew what to do to get my game back and start shooting low and winning some cash. I had spent two superb weeks working with my coach David Whelan at the David Leadbetter Academy in Florida. The weather was great and I was playing without pressure, working on all aspects of my game for seven or eight hours a day. Everything just fell into place.

So when I flew to Cape Town for my first tournament of the season, I was feeling so confident it was ridiculous. My whole game was excellent. I could hit any type of shot I wanted at will. It was all so easy. I was so eager because I felt I was playing the best golf of my life.

When I went to South Africa I honestly believed I was ready to win a tournament. The trouble was I had spent two whole weeks working on technique. I had forgotten to switch off so when the heat was on I was thinking technically - which is what I now know psychologists call 'using your left brain.' That's always been a problem of mine, thinking about technique. So from the first day of the South African Open I was playing with swing thoughts on the course again and that destroyed my confidence.

I played awful and shot 73 and 74. I remember asking myself what was the point in going to the States and spending all that money. I might just as well have stayed home and enjoyed Christmas and New Year with my friends and family.

So it shows how fleeting confidence can be. It had all gone wrong because on the course I was worrying how my swing was looking rather than just playing the game of golf.

The following week I went to Johannesburg but my confidence was shattered. Now I couldn't even hit the ball on the range let alone on the course in front of 10,000 people. I was performing pathetically and I could not figure out why. I telephoned across the Atlantic asking my coach what had gone wrong but he couldn't help. My problem was in my mind, not in my grip or set-up or takeaway. And inside my head was where I found the solution with the help of Dr. John Pates.

We solved it on the range together. Dr. John taught me to abandon these swing thoughts and recall great shots I had hit when things were going well in Florida. I imagined myself making a perfect swing on a television screen, focusing on the target and then letting go. It was that simple. I'd made several video recordings of myself swinging perfectly and hitting awesome shots in the States so all I had to do was see that picture in my mind and walk into myself, walk into that perfect swing as though I was inside the television screen knowing that I could not fail, that I would repeat this perfect swing. We call this 'shot recollection.'

A particular favourite of mine back then was a shot I pulled off in the States. It was on a long par five and I hit this perfect three-wood about 250 yards, drifting off the left-hand side onto the green, with just a hint of fade through a narrow entrance, and rolling to within 12 feet of the pin.

So in my mind I wasn't on the range in Johannesburg, I was back in Florida making this perfect swing with a perfect result, the best swing I had ever made in my life. All those emotions came back to me as I switched from technical mode to playing mode. My confidence came flooding back. I made the cut in Johannesburg and I could sense a good performance was just around the corner. I had completely reconditioned myself.

The following week I went to Singapore and finished in the top 10 after a last round of 68. I had been way off track just two weeks before and what was killing me was my natural tendency to play technically, something I had always struggled with as an amateur and throughout my early career as a professional. The week in Johannesburg was a transitional period when I was building my confidence back. I left there thinking I had got my game back again. I was starting to play well.

The first two rounds at Johannesburg I was beating the demons away and I struggled to make the cut. I had to work hard to stop myself from getting bogged down in swing thoughts. That freed me up and at the weekend I really committed myself to the new process and made a solid finish. So I flew to Singapore with my confidence sky high. My success there was all down to my work with Dr. John on the range in Johannesburg when I recreated images of my perfect swing inside my mind.

My experiences prove that I hadn't actually lost my confidence. It had always been there, within me, but I had forgotten how to access it. Everyone slips in and out of feeling confident. You can see it on the Tour every week. That's the way all our minds work, just like yours.

Think what it would be like if confidence was a tangible thing you could feel and see, like the petrol you use to run your car. Think how good it would be to fill up your confidence before you play as if you were a car running low on fuel, dropping in on a garage to fill up your tank of confidence.

Well now you can. And Dr. John can show you how.

How to Develop Confidence

Dr. John

I was lecturing at Sheffield Hallam University when I met Darren Clarke. He was the first golfer I worked with you could really call a superstar. Peter Cowan, who coached Darren and Lee Westwood, among others, had invited me to the 2002 English Open at the Forest of Arden.

You probably know that the day before most European Tour events a Pro-Am is held. This low-key competition is an opportunity for sponsors to enjoy rubbing shoulders with some of the world's leading players. Professionals use this round to fine tune their knowledge of the course and though performing well is not important to them, they do not like playing badly 24 hours before the actual competition. Darren shot 84, an unbelievably bad round considering he was one of the best players in the world.

He had not won a tournament for almost a year. Darren was down. He was depressed and running out of ideas.

Pete Cowan asked me to see Darren. He said he thought my ideas might help him. Peter said Darren had lost his confidence and he didn't know how to get it back. I met Darren in his hotel room on the Wednesday night before the tournament began. We chatted for three hours to assess his problems and give me an opportunity to help him think in a more positive way.

His mind was in a bit of a mess, to be honest, but I was familiar with the problem. I had come across the same negative way of thinking with other golfers. Every time Darren was about to hit a shot all he could think about were bad swings. He was swamping himself with the worst possible images. This is a common fault among players in a slump. We soon found a solution.

It was great working with Darren. He's a quick learner who is great at imagery. So what should have been strength had become a weakness. He was using his imagery skills to recall bad shots and that was destroying him.

Golfers everywhere often do that. I'm sure you've seen your pals talk this way. You've probably slipped into this habit occasionally yourself, no matter how well you have played. Pros are the same. Every week on Tour I see players come into the clubhouse after shooting five or six-under and talk about one missed putt or a poor bunker shot or a bad drive that cost them a bogey. They are never satisfied. So they focus on bad shots.

There's a pattern here. Often players play one bad shot and then focus on it during the actual round. So one bogey is often followed by another, then another and before long, what should have been a 66 or 67 becomes a 73.

The opposite is also true. When a player hits a great shot, say a three-wood close to the pin on a long, tight par five, that often leads to a string of birdies. I've researched this and it's incredible how often this happens. The only thing that is different is how they think. Their swings do not alter but their minds do.

That kind of profile is common among some of the world's top players. Colin Montgomerie is a classic example. His scorecards are often littered with strings of bogeys or birdies and it's easy to pinpoint when he hit a particularly poor shot or when he turned on the magic, as we all know he can.

In his previous tournaments Darren was constantly following one bad shot with a couple of bogeys – it was almost guaranteed. Concentrating on bad shots causes you to immediately slip into the wrong mental state to play well. That happens more or less instantaneously on the golf course. That's a short-term problem. Long-term though, that kind of thinking is really serious because over time, say several weeks, it will start to erode your confidence. Then you're in a slump.

I asked Darren to think of a time when he was playing well, when he hit the ball perfectly, holed putts and won a tournament. He chose his 2000 World Matchplay Championship victory over Tiger Woods when he played magnificently at the La Costa Golf Club in California.

It was easy for Darren because even though the best part of two years had gone by, the memory was clear to him, as if it was yesterday. He could remember every hole and every shot of that 36-hole final. We started on the first tee, completing the first hole and moved on to the second. All the detail was there in his mind – what part of the fairway he was in, where Tiger Woods' ball was and even some of the conversation he had held with his caddy and what they were thinking at different times during the final.

He had the perfect mental game that day. Darren told me what it was like when Woods kept hitting the ball 20 yards beyond his tee shot. He said it was no problem to him because deep down he was supremely confident of putting his next shot on the green first, close to the pin. It was as if he was saying to Tiger: 'Follow that.'

In his mind, Darren relived the wonderful feeling he had when he holed the putt that won him the championship, fairly comfortably on the 15th green. He recalled Tiger congratulating him, how the crowd cheered – all wonderful, positive memories.

He looked at me, beaming with confidence, a broad smile across his face. I reminded him how powerful thinking that way was and that he needed to use the same imagery skills tomorrow in the tournament. That would get him in the right emotional state to help him play. I guaranteed that.

Darren had begun to recognise the feeling that recounting great memories can give him. I asked him to make associations with other thoughts that could reproduce this incredible sensation. We discovered that music worked particularly well for Darren. He was fond of the theme tune to Sylvester Stallone's *Rocky* movies called *The Eye Of The Tiger*. The tune is loud and aggressive and the catchy melody gave him a similar emotional response to hitting a good shot.

Music works with most people. Like all art, it taps into your emotions very quickly. We've all experienced the benefits of music, haven't we? I have often played a favourite CD and by the time the song has finished, my state of mind is totally different. It only takes a couple of minutes, perhaps less. Usually I become happy. Music puts us into a good mood. Art is a fantastic way of expressing emotions and creating positive feelings – confidence, enjoyment, high energy and excitement. If you know how to tap into them you can get yourself into the correct mental state to play your best golf.

Go to a place that you feel comfortable in your mind. Darren went back to La Costa Golf Club in California, where he pulled off his momentous defeat of Tiger Woods. For you it might be your local course on a day when you played particularly well. Give it some thought. All the shots will be there inside your head; it's just a question of digging them out.

We worked on Darren's memories throughout his career and made them specific to a particular club, filtering through tens of thousands of shots, discarding the mediocre, the average, the good, even the very good until all we had left were perfect shots. I remember the emotional thought Darren used when he hit his driver at the Forest of Arden was an opening tee shot at Wentworth in the PGA Championships the year before. Everything about that shot was perfect - the timing, the rhythm and the strike. Then he would imagine he was listening to the *Eye Of The Tiger* as if he had a CD player in his head. Finally, when he was over the ball, I asked him to focus on the target, whatever that might have been. If you are playing to a pin, the visualisation will be easier than if you are hitting towards a featureless fairway. That doesn't matter. In your mind, stick a flag or a bright post where you want the ball to go. Your mind can do anything to distort reality and get you in the right frame of mind. Try it. So now Darren is ready to hit the ball and with all those positive thoughts flooding into his brain he is virtually certain of a good shot. And that's what happened in the tournament.

Darren also used the progressive relaxation techniques we have talked about in another chapter. Do you remember Gary Emerson in the Italian Open and how he squeezed his club? Well Darren did the same thing and it was just as successful.

We had enjoyed our time together. Darren was an easy pupil who opened his mind up to my ideas. And as I have already told you, he has amazing powers of imagery. I wished him well and I had a strong feeling he was going to play well. He did too.

He shot 65 in the first round, an astonishing reduction of 19 shots. Darren followed that with three more great scores of 70, 68 and 68 for a final total of 17-under to win the tournament by three shots from Soren Hansen, the Danish player.

Remember, Darren did not have a new putter or a new driver. He had not altered his swing or changed his ball or his caddy. No, all Darren had done was to think smart.

I must say I wasn't surprised when Darren asked me to be his sports psychologist for the rest of the season. His improvement had been spectacular and unexpected and caused quite a stir in the golfing media. Two days later I was in New York assisting Darren in the US Open, which was being played on the horrendously difficult Bethpage Park course on the outskirts of New York. I remember Darren played his practice rounds with Thomas Bjorn. It was an incredible experience for me walking inside the ropes with these two great players. Darren continued with the process and played well, finishing in the top 24 with a host of big-name players behind him. I remember one particular shot he played in the practice round. He pulled his tee shot on the difficult par three 17th, and he was on the edge of the green but a long way left, perhaps 40 feet. The pin position and the severe slope compounded the difficulty of the shot. It was virtually impossible to get the ball within 20 feet. Darren aimed away from the flag, hit the putt and it went in. There were more than 5,000 fans there and they went mad. The shot was featured on CNN on American television that night as the shot of the day. It was an incredible experience being part of that and knowing that his improved form was primarily down to smart thinking.

Summary

If you are not confident you will never play well. It's impossible. Fred Couples' technique was simple – he always remembered his best shots. So build up a library of shots with all your clubs. Recall a great tee shot or a long putt or a holed bunker shot. Whatever your handicap is, you will have played well and hit a stack of good shots in your career. Get into the feelings and excitement of the emotions you were feeling when you hit the shot. Another technique that will help you is music.

The great Sam Snead played every shot he ever hit with an orchestra playing a waltz inside his head. I'm sure that was one of the reasons he swung the club with such wonderful timing. Then you must focus on positive outcomes. For Darren, this was his victory over Tiger Woods. You might have a vivid memory of a club medal or a friendly you played in with your pals when you took the money and played really well. The principle is the same. You will be in the right emotional state and I guarantee you will be much more likely to play your best golf and fulfil your dreams. I'm not saying it's going to be easy.

You can start to build up these memories in bed, in the car or when you are on holiday. Remember, Darren Clarke went from 84 to 65 in 24 hours. Use the same techniques as Darren and you can feel confident whenever you want.

CHAPTER THREE

Staying in the Present

Dean

I'm going to tell you two stories about my experiences trying to qualify for the British Open. They illustrate perfectly how important it is to stay in the present when you are close to achieving your goals on the golf course.

Let's begin by going back to 1992 when I was still an amateur. The Open that year was at Muirfield - you may recall Nick Faldo went on to win by one shot from American Dr. John Cook. My final qualifying round was at Gullane, not far from Muirfield. It is an exceptionally difficult course and with a strong wind blowing, my first round 71 put me in the top seven and in with a great chance of playing in the big one as there were 12 places up for grabs. There were a lot of good players at Gullane, among them European Tour stars such as Peter Mitchell and Per-Ulrick Johansson.

It was a two-round competition and my competitors' badge allowed me free entry to Muirfield to watch the practice day. I made a big mistake going to Muirfield because my visit there naturally got me thinking about what it would mean to me, to play in this great tournament as an amateur.

Back then I was a competent player with a proven track record of winning amateur events and shooting low numbers. I was confident. But as I walked along the first fairway at Muirfield, soaking in the atmosphere and watching all my heroes like Jack Nicklaus, Tom Watson, Sandy Lyle and Seve Ballesteros, it started to dawn on me what I was close to achieving. And here, at the course, my dreams seemed so real I could almost reach out and touch them.

I know now that my visit to Muirfield was precisely the worst thing I could possibly do. I went back to my hotel in North Berwick with my mind spinning and when I woke up the next day to prepare for my final round, I looked out of the window and the trees were touching the ground. It was a howling gale and I knew it was going to be a day for solid golf and good course management, all the attributes I went to the course thinking I had. But the damage had been done. I couldn't get Muirfield out of my head and I was unable to get back to doing what I did best - playing in the present and executing a game plan.

I was flying so high. At first things went well and I thought I could handle the situation. On the practice range I hit the ball perfectly and everything was set up for a good finish. So here I am standing on the first tee looking down the fairway at this driveable par four, with the wind blasting from my left.

Well, I took out my driver having calculated that was the shot to hit and bang, away went the ball, so far right it was not only out-of-bounds, it carried a road, a large house, some gardens and landed on the top of someone's roof. I had to reload and all of a sudden I became afraid and nervous as I could see my dream being blown away in front of me. If memory serves I went on to shoot 85. The day was a complete disaster. And the reason was simple. I was too busy concerning myself with the excitement of playing in the Open, the biggest tournament in the world.

So thinking about outcomes had destroyed me. Now I want to tell you about a similar experience which had a happy ending when I qualified to play in the 2000 Open Championship at St Andrews. Eight years on from Gullane, I had become a seasoned campaigner on the European Tour. I had played in three Opens and made the cut in two. In 1995 I played at St Andrews when Dr. John Daly took the title, two years later I was at Royal Troon when Justin Leonard was the champion and then at Carnoustie in 1999 when Jean Van De Velde had his problems on 18 to allow Paul Lawrie to lift the old claret jug.

I was trying to qualify at Lundin Links and in the first round I shot 69, which was OK but left me needing to shoot low to get into the main tournament. I knew my second round had to be seven or eight under to make it.

My playing partners were Paul Casey and Paul Stankowski, who were off the pace. But I knew I had a chance. I was six-under with two to play but I made a dreadful three-putt bogey, which put me back on the cut-line. As I walked off the 17th green, word reached me that there was a big play-off waiting to start on the first tee. There were loads of players for just a couple of spots. I didn't want any of that. I wanted to qualify by right.

Things did not start start too well on the 18th when I hit a poor drive into the wind. Those of you who have played Lundin Links will know what a tough hole it is. There's out-of-bounds all the way up the left and again close to the green - there seems to be white posts everywhere.

I can still remember the exact yardage my caddie gave me - 257 yards to the pin. We were in the final group and I had to wait for the players in front to finish. While I was waiting an official told me what I needed to do. It was simple - a par would earn me a place in the play-offs, a birdie and I'd be in the Open, a bogey and I was history. Just for a moment I started to think about outcomes and how tough it would be to par the hole from this position and what it would mean to me to play at St Andrews.

I was a different player then than I was in 1993. I had mental strength and I knew what to do so I was able to ignore these thoughts and stay in the present, focusing on my routine and mental relaxation, thinking of a perfect shot I had hit with the club I was about to use, which was a three-wood.

I'm not saying I wasn't nervous at Lundin Links. Who wouldn't be? But while I was waiting, even though there was a lot at stake and I was faced with one of the toughest shots of my life, I controlled the situation because I wasn't there. My mind had taken me on a mental voyage to a beautiful beach in Barbados where I had spent a wonderful holiday recently, away from all the tension and all the pressure.

In my mind I could picture the palm trees and this relaxation did the trick.

The group ahead are walking off the green and my caddy hands me the three-wood bringing me 4,000 miles back in an instant away from the beach and back to East Scotland where the most important shot of my life was waiting for me.

I visualised the shot and picked the target I wanted, a specific target, nothing vague like the green. I picked out a white out-of-bounds post on exactly the line we calculated the ball needed to start on. But white wasn't strong enough so I pressed an imaginery key inside my head and it's not white anymore, the post has changed to bright red, orange even, like the brightest fire engine I had ever seen. I went on one last journey, up into the sky as if I was Peter Pan, looking down on the green making it look big, so big I felt I couldn't miss it, taking one last look at myself down the fairway, alongside my caddy holding the club in my hand, ready to go.

I'm back over the ball now, that orange post shining brightly inside my mind and the ball's away, the best shot I have ever hit in my life. It was perfect in every way, a soft draw just as I had visualised that landed just short of the green, rolling up to within 15 feet of the pin. But I wasn't home yet.

The putt was a right-to-left breaker, uphill, a cup and a half to the right. I went through the same routine of mental relaxation, totally blanking out the enormity of the putt in front of me.

I thought of a similar putt I had holed earlier in the round, accessing those feelings, reliving how I felt when the putt dropped, visualising the stroke in my mind. I went through my routine, pulled the trigger and in it went, straight in the middle and there I was off to St Andrews. It was fantastic feeling. I was ecstatic.

I went on to finish 26th in the tournament playing with Pierre Fulke in the first two rounds and Sergio Garcia on the last two days. But it gets even better.

I was due to play a practice round on Wednesday with Gary Orr and the defending champion Paul Lawrie. So

I'm on the putting green waiting to tee off and my caddy comes running up to me really excited.

"Dean, Dean," he said. "Do you want to move up? The Darce has pulled out."

The Darce is the Irish golfer Eamonn Darcy. I told him we had a match already arranged. I couldn't understand him.

"No Dean. There's a gap now and you'll be playing with Christy O'Connor Junior, Dr. John Daly and Jack Nicklaus."

"OK. We're there." I said, as quickly as I could.

I was shaking like a leaf. I was spellbound and totally in awe. Practice rounds are really laborious but that didn't bother me. Jack and Dr. John were fantastic.

All the way round, they were telling us how they had won Opens there and where they played certain shots from. It was an incredible experience I will never forget. What a thrill it was when Jack Nicklaus shook my hand on the 18th green and thanked me for the game.

It had been one of the greatest days of my life. But it was only possible because I had stayed in the present on the 18th fairway at Lundin Links and pulled off that amazing three-wood shot I will never forget.

Staying in the Present

Dr. John

This is a classic problem for all golfers from the best players in the world to novices playing in their first competition. In the golfing sense, thinking about outcomes means thinking about your final score, concentrating on birdieing the next three holes, worrying about your final place in the tournament, and thinking about how many shots you can cut off your handicap.

The first thing to recognise is that outcomes are out of your control. You could play the best golf of your life in the club championships and shoot 65 only to be beaten by a lower score. Does that mean you have played badly? Of course not.

If you focus on outcomes you are guaranteed to struggle with your confidence. Your stress levels will go up. Say you are a five-handicapper and you shoot six-over, if you are outcome orientated, you will be likely to interpret that score negatively. You will think you have failed, which is a bit ridiculous. You've probably played really well.

I lot of Tour players I talk to struggle with this. If they don't shoot well under par, they often assume they are failures. They start to think they aren't good enough to be on Tour and the next thing you know they have no confidence and struggle to get their game back.

The only thing you can control on a golf course is yourself. That means many things but primarily you must bombard yourself with positive emotions. That will get you in your zone and you will be highly likely to shoot a good score.

How about making your goal to get in your zone? Or to get in a relaxed state over every shot? They are called process goals and the difference is you can control them but you obviously can't control every other golfer in the tournament, the weather, your playing partners or if your ball gets a bad kick into an unplayable lie in a bunker.

Processed and performance goals are under your control – they are measurable, manageable and they can give you enormous confidence. Don't try to shoot a particular score. Don't try to win a tournament. Don't try to beat a particular player. Those are major outcome goals that will frustrate you.

When I first started working with Dean Robertson he had missed a few cuts. Then he went on to make nine from his next ten events and virtually secured his Tour card for another season. Not long after I met Dean, I remember him playing in Cape Town, South Africa and he was two-under par with three holes to play in the second round. He had made a dramatic improvement in the way he was thinking on the golf course but then, without warning, on the 16th tee he became outcome orientated. He started to think about birdieing the last three holes and contemplating how much he would rise up the leaderboard and how much money he might win. He bogeyed all three and missed the cut by one.

Steve Gallacher is another player who was stuck in a rut thinking about outcomes he could not control. When he focuses on playing well he is a different person to when he starts thinking about making cuts, top 10 finishes and winning tournaments.

Steve plays his best when he picks the club, selects a target, keeps that in his mind and hits the ball. It's that simple. Focusing on your target prevents you from thinking about outcomes. You can't evaluate anything.

If you hit the ball left, right or straight down the fairway – so what. You have to hit your next shot anyway. So instead of worrying, say about being in a bunker or in the rough change the way you think. Instead of thinking you might leave the ball in the bunker or fail to get the ball out of the rough, look at your next shot as a challenge. Enjoy the difficulty. Improve your short game because if you fancy your chances of getting up and down if you miss the green that will take all the pressure off. Then the tension will go and you'll start hitting more greens because you will be focusing on the target and not on the bad places your ball might go.

You need to keep faith with a pre-shot routine that allows your mind to be consumed with processes that enable you to get into your zone. We've talked about these elements many times – relaxation, confidence, excitement, positive emotions such as fun and focusing on the target. If you do that your scores will come tumbling down.

Summary

Forget about outcomes and find the keys to your own personal zone, that wonderful place your mind can take you, that will allow you to play your best golf. Focusing on your keys, on your positive emotions, will amplify them and make them more powerful. Use your mind to unlock the power of imagery, think what it would be like to be inside the body of Tiger Woods, to swing like him in an Open Championship.

Imagine your own television screen inside your head and put in as much detail as you can – the crowd, the noise, the colour and the atmosphere.

Build your own private library of images so draw on whenever your need them. All the great champions can help you – and when you start thinking like them, you just might start playing like them.

CHAPTER FOUR

Never Think about Technique on the Course

Dean

When I started working with Dr. John Pates I had made only one cut out of my last eight tournaments on the European Tour. I needed help. The trouble was I couldn't figure out where I was going wrong. I was hitting the ball wonderfully on the range yet I couldn't take it onto the course. I just couldn't score. Now I know my problems were all coming from the way I was thinking. I was using my 'left brain,' which is about movement and co-ordination when I should have been using my 'right brain' which is artistic and creative. That's the way most of us try to play this game. Swing thoughts are comfortable to us but thinking that way will nearly always destroy your score rather than help you. I'll try to illustrate for you the enormous benefit that forgetting about technique on the course made for me and what you can learn from my roller coaster performance in Switzerland a couple of years ago.

The change was dramatic and instantaneous, almost as quick as turning a light on and off, one moment confusion and frustration, the next I was focusing positively and knocking the pins out. After missing cut after cut I went on to make nine cuts in the next ten tournaments and the only thing I altered was the way I thought. I stopped thinking technically and began focusing on feelings and targets. I played with more freedom and I actually started having fun on the course.

A great example of the power of changing the way you think was in the 2002 Omega European Masters at Crans-sur-Sierre in Switzerland. I played with the eventual winner Robert Karlsson in the first two rounds. Robert won the event on 14-under-par, four shots ahead of my fellow countryman and friend Paul Lawrie and South African Trevor Immelman. Although I was just returning to the Tour after a lay-off my preparation had been perfect. I was relaxed and expecting to play well.

I had been practising in Tenerife and over in the States with my coach David Whelan and my whole game was spot on. My practice rounds had gone well and I was full of confidence, enthusiasm and excitement. Yet inexplicably I shot a disastrous 79. There seemed to be no explanation for how badly I had played. I've looked back at the records and I had four double bogeys that day, that's eight shots gone in just four holes. I finished the day 152nd out of a field of 156, with four guys I'd never heard of behind me.

One of my swing thoughts back then was rotation of the clubface in the backswing. It was magic on the driving range. That thought produced a great feeling and rhythm yet it was the very thing that went on to destroy me in the tournament.

I wasn't thinking about the target or where I wanted the ball to go … I was concentrating on exactly where the clubface was in the backswing.

And the more I tried to think this way the worse my shots became. Back then I thought that my problem was technical and the solution was to concentrate more on getting the clubface into this theoretical position. It's hard to believe now. I was concentrating on the very thing that was holding me back which is like trying to put out a fire by throwing petrol onto the blaze.

It gets worse. I wasn't just thinking about the clubface during my actual shots, I continued going through various drills on the side of the tee or on the fairway, desperate to figure out what was wrong. I was even concentrating on this on the putting green, practising my backswing while the other players walked around the green. It was crazy.

So I struggled along to the 16th, which had been redesigned by Seve Ballesteros the previous year. It had been a short par four but now it was a par three which I call the only dogleg par three in the world. The hole is super-tough, 236 yards through a small gap in tall pine trees. My caddy and I picked a 2-iron which was the right club given the fact that we were at altitude.

So I get on the tee with this 2-iron thinking only one thing, getting the clubface rotating perfectly. You won't be surprised when I tell you the result was a half-shank, which veered way to the right and smashed into a tree before bouncing back towards the tee. I think I finished with a five which pretty much summed up the day.

I left the 18th green and arranged to meet Dr. John immediately and within 30 seconds he told me where I had gone wrong. He told me to stop thinking about 'rotating the clubface' and to move into the 'right brain.' It was pretty simple stuff. So I prepared for a better performance the next day by thinking smart.

I knew that after a 79 it would take an incredible round for me to make the cut. That took the pressure off, though believe it or not, I still felt that I could do it. One thing was certain. I wasn't going to make a good score thinking technically. I had to start visualising and thinking about targets – not about swing mechanics. I had a great big 79 on my mind to prove how dangerous it was to think that way.

So with the help of Dr. John I moved from left brain thinking to right brain thinking which allowed me to play with freedom and creativity. I had fun and hit a lot of greens and made a few putts. I remember having a great start and gathering momentum quickly before going on to shoot 66, a difference of 13 shots which is vast for a tournament professional – the difference between a Lamborghini and a Ford Fiesta with a broken engine. There were only two 65s that day, from Andrew Coltart and Englishman Matthew Cort. So on the first day 151 players beat my score and on the second day, when my mind was right, only two players shot lower than me.

To be honest, even now, looking back, the change surprises me and emphasises how powerful your mind is if you want to play your best. The conditions were exactly the same both days – a light breeze in ideal temperatures. I did not have a new driver or a new putter, just a new mind or rather a new way of thinking which allowed me to focus on what really matters – the target. So a reduction of 13 shots in less than 24 hours just by thinking correctly is pretty amazing.

I used a range of techniques that day to help me shoot five-under but the one I found worked particularly well in the second round was visualisation. During my pre-shot routine I looked at myself externally using an imaginary TV. This is how I made it work.

It was as if I had a television and video recorder along-side every tee and fairway. Before every shot I imagined switching on the TV and pressing the play button, seeing myself make a perfect swing, the swings I had been making all week on the practice round. Everything was exactly as I wanted it to be in my imaginary world, the best swing I had ever made in my life every time, fault-less, technically perfect with a smooth rhythm. Even the clubface rotation that had destroyed me in the first round was exactly right.

I remember the week before enjoying a particularly good video lesson I'd had with my coach David Whelan in Tenerife when I was swinging the club awesome. So on my imaginary TV screen I watched myself swinging. There I was, wearing the same red T-shirt on the same range, the ball arrowing towards the flag without effort. The image was clear and powerful.

So I fixed this image in my mind, not vaguely and without feeling but strongly with great conviction, making the technique strong and creating massive confi-dence as though it was impossible for me to deviate from that perfect swing.

Then I switched off the TV and started focusing on the target, whatever that was at the time. It might have been a tree, or a flag or a corner of the green. The important thing was to drop every thought about technique and replace it with a picture in my mind of where I wanted the ball to go as if I was placing co-ordinates into a computer that would guide a missile to its target.

Some players find it difficult to concentrate on targets, especially when they are a long way away or don't stand out enough. But your mind can do that for you by changing reality. Make the target bigger, frame it in your mind, make the flag a different colour, say like an orange fire engine or move the flag in your mind so it's on a driving range you are comfortable with.

So even though I might be looking at the ball I still had a clear image of the target in my mind's eye. I was seeing the only thing that mattered which was the target. It's like throwing snowballs when you're a growing up. If you want to hit one of your pals you home in on them, on the target. If you're eight years old you aren't going to think about the angle your arm needs to be or snapping your wrist at the right time, are you? Of course not. Children don't think like that. They focus on the target, on their pals, and most of the time they will hit them.

Then children grow up and start playing golf and reading magazines and having lessons. So they forget what they did instinctively when they were children.

So I know all too well the dangers of thinking about technique on the course. I will never make the same mistake again. I hope you won't either.

Never Think about Technique on the Course

Dr. John

Trying to work on your swing when you are on the golf course is one of the most destructive things you can do. There are logical reasons for this. We all want to improve and usually that means working on our technique with a good coach. That's an important aspect but you have to know when and where to work on technique – and that should never be on the golf course.

When you play or practise golf, you should use either your learning head or your playing head. They are completely different and you must keep them separate. If you are on the practice ground or the range, working on technical improvements you will be thinking primarily, though not exclusively, using your learning head. But on the course, whether you are in an important tournament or just playing with your pals for a few beers, your priority will be to complete your round in the fewest shots. Then you must have your playing head on. If you slip into technical thoughts, you're finished and it is virtually impossible to play well.

Can you remember when England were losing to Greece in a World Cup qualifier at Old Trafford a few years ago? You may recall David Beckham scoring an equaliser with a spectacular free kick from the edge of the penalty area in injury time to level the score 2-2.

He was under incredible pressure. If he failed, England missed out on automatic qualification for the World Cup and faced the uncertainty of the play-offs. There were 70,000 fans watching him and millions more live on television across the country. The whole nation was relying on Beckham. But he handled that pressure to launch a wonderful shot into the top left hand corner of the net and become a national hero.

Do you think he was thinking of the angle of his foot or the number of steps he was taking or if his arms were pointing in a certain direction? Of course not. He focused on the target, relaxed and let go, very much like we do when we play our best golf. Beckham scored because he did what came natural to him. If he had thought of technique I'm sure he would have missed. You must play golf in the same way by allowing your subconscious to take over.

We call this right brain control. When we learn a skill through repetition we perform the task more efficiently when we don't think. When you are over the ball, try to imagine that there is a lever inside your head controlling your thoughts. See the target, focus on it, and then mentally switch off and think of nothing. You will definitely hit the ball better whatever the shot, whether it is a full drive to a tight fairway or a three-foot putt.

I admit golfers struggle to think this way. It does not come naturally to us. Believe me, Tour professionals are just as bad as the rest of us. They try to control their swings and prevent their subconscious from taking control. There's something about swing thoughts that are comfortable to us. That's the way we learnt the game and it's a tough habit to kick.

When you play on the course using your learning head, your attention is on technical movements such as swing planes, takeaway or clubhead position, when what you should be doing is concentrating on targets and where you want the ball to go. Technical thinking on the course will destroy your performance.

Your distance control and accuracy will be terrible and it's virtually guaranteed that you will score badly. Let's be clear on what you are trying to achieve on the golf course - completing your round in the fewest shots.

When you play on the course, especially in important competitions, you should be trying to get into that mental bubble we have referred to so many times, a magical place, where you can soak up the positive feelings that will allow you to play your best golf. You should also be very target focused. If you clutter your mind with swing thoughts, all your instinctive feelings will be suppressed and you will rely on the skills you employed to learn the swing, which are not appropriate to scoring.

Look back and try to remember what is on your mind whenever you play well. I'll bet your mind is a blank. Golf is easy and you don't have to try to play well. It just happens. Everything is effortless and you automatically hit the ball well, think clearly and hole a few putts - that is probably because you are in a cocoon of concentration where you focus on the target, on where you want the ball to go. The best swing thought you can have on the course is a blank mind - that would be perfect.

Masters champion Ian Woosnam has employed one simple mental technique since he first joined the Tour more than 20 years ago - ball and divot. Yes, it's that simple. And it works. So if you need any encouragement to follow his tip, just look at his record – 1991 Masters Champion and winner of more than 40 tournaments. He's that good.

Ian focuses on the strike because to him, that's the important part. For Ian, the ball just gets in the way of his wonderful swing. He's like a metronome - ball, divot - ball, divot - ball, divot - and that's one of the prime reasons why Ian has been one of the world's greatest players for more than two decades. Ian never thinks about his swing so if that's good enough for a former world number one, it must be right for the rest of us.

So we have established that if you go onto the course to work on your swing you are unlikely to play very well. You are not allowing your swing to be automatic. The only way you can achieve that is by not thinking during the second or so it takes to complete your swing. If you try to consciously control the movement, you will lose rhythm, speed and tempo. Then you will be out of sync and as a consequence, start rattling up the sixes and sevens that will destroy your card.

Next time you are on the driving range I want you to try something that will prove the value of my advice. Hit a couple of shots by replicating the way you play most of the time, by concentrating on technique and swing positions. Make a mental note of how successful you are. Then try this. Make your mind blank apart from one image - the target. And here's how to do it.

Firstly, align yourself to your target. Just before you are about to hit the ball, look up and see the target - let's say a flag 150 yards away. In your mind, imagine you have a theoretical camera inside your brain - click, take a picture and retain the image in your mind - make it powerful and clear. You may want to take a moving image so the process is the same but this time picture a video camera and see the flag fluttering in the distance. Press the record button for five seconds and think of a TV screen showing the image clearly and without distraction. Now keep those images in your mind when you come back to the ball, erase all other thoughts and hit the shot.

I know this is a difficult concept so I will try to help you. When I suggest this to players for the first time, they find it difficult because they can't retain that image in their brain once they actually look away from the target - when they stare at the ball they see the ball when I want them to see the target. They say the image of the target fades instantaneously and as they take the clubhead away, their natural instinct is to think technically.

So you have to learn how to keep the target in your head when you are looking at the ball, a moment before your swing starts. All the great players do this. You can too. You have to control the image by changing it, by making the picture even more powerful than reality. It's a special technique called 'changing the sub-modality'. You can alter focus, movement, size and colour.

Remember we are assuming your target is a flag but it can be anything – a tree, a post, a building or a cloud. The process is still the same. You can start by altering the colour of the flag. If it's yellow you might not find that particular colour pleasing to you. It might not be bright enough. So change it. You might want to make it red, the colour of a fire engine or a postbox. So after you've made it the brightest colour you can imagine, concentrate on the movement as it flutters in the wind, but exaggerate it, make it shake violently and in your mind create a theoretical flag that is bigger and dominates your image. In reality the flag is a long way away and surrounded by green fairway and other similar flags. But in your mind you are distorting reality and making it big, imposing and colourful so your mind has a distinct and simple target to aim for. Vagueness has been replaced by clarity. That's the power of your mind.

Now imagine the sound the flag is making in your theoretical world as your theoretical wind moves the fabric violently. The image is ten times more powerful than reality and you are 100 times more likely to focus on it. If you can do this, when you look at the ball you will still see the only thing that matters - the target.

I guarantee that you are more likely to hit the ball where you want it to go. There are scientific reasons for this that are connected with how your mind works. Your brain is like the computer inside a technologically perfect missile. If you programme a missile to hit a vague target like, say, Scotland, it probably won't get there. If you target St Andrews the chances are increased, if you target the Old Course, it will increase again and finally, if you tell it to hit the clock tower on the Old Course club house it will. Your mind works the same way.

When you focus on technique on the course you are underplaying the most important thing, which is the target. So if you hit in the vague direction of the fairway or the green, the ball can go anywhere. You can stop that happening by focusing on the flag and making it dominant in your mind. If there isn't a flag to aim for, put one there. Think only of the image - not swing thoughts.

I first met Steve Gallacher in Italy and even though he is incredibly talented he had only just made his Tour card that year, for the second year running. We worked on the range before he teed off and I figured out immediately what was hurting him. Steve could not stop thinking about technique on the golf course. It was destroying him. That was the way he had always played. It was comfortable to him but he soon realised that my advice was right.

We worked on targets and he was so impressed he decided to use the techniques that day, in the actual tournament. He was two-over after four holes but he kept concentrating on the image of the target to shoot nine-under for the next 14 holes, his best score of the year. What better testimony can you have than that.

Summary

Remember, you play golf in two different ways - learning and playing. You will struggle to achieve long-term improvement without working on technique - I'm not saying that technique is not important. So find a good coach and work on your swing on the range, but not on the course. When you go out onto the course, especially in a competition, you must switch off your learning head and use your playing head.

All your energies should be used to focus on playing the game and completing the round in the fewest shots. This means getting in the right emotional state to play the shot, and using a mental pre-shot routine that will encourage you to focus on the target. If you think technically, by using swing thoughts, it will take all your concentration away from what really matters.

I will permit you to have one swing thought, but it must be an image, not a technical position. Think of the most perfect swing you have ever made or imagine yourself inside the body of Ernie Els when he makes that glorious athletic movement of his to send the ball 300 yards down the fairway. See it on that internal television you have inside your head.

Imagery will allow your subconscious to take control and hit the shot freely, just like David Beckham does every week playing for Real Madrid.

CHAPTER FIVE

How to Get in the Right
Mood to Play your Best Golf

Dean

The single most important feeling you need on the golf course is relaxation. I use physical and mental relaxation techniques to achieve this. I produce confidence by recalling situations when I have played my best golf. I access associations with great times on and off the course to make me confident.

I represented Scotland in the 2001 World Cup of Golf at The Taiheiyo Club in Shizouka, Japan. My partner was Andrew Coltart and in the third round we were playing four-ball format, which means pars are not so good. You need to shoot birdies and plenty of them. So there was a lot of pressure on us. As if that wasn't enough, we were drawn to play with Tiger Woods and David Duval.

Tiger was the US Masters champion and Duval was the British Open champion after a sensational victory at Royal Lytham & St Annes. Following Tiger's victory at Augusta, he held all four Major championship trophies having won The British Open, the US Open and the US PGA titles in 2000. David was obviously one of the world's greatest players, his status in the game high-lighted with a final round 59 in 1999 when he eagled the last hole to win the Bob Hope Chrysler Classic.

We were the second last group out and there are 35,000 Japanese fans all over the course trying to get a glimpse of Tiger. They were ecstatic, excited and enthu-siastic at the thought of following this golfing god.

So there's Andrew and myself on the first tee trying to compose ourselves surrounded by all this hype. I'm sure you can imagine how nervous we were. We had both experienced plenty of pressure situations before but nothing like this. It was amazing.

This was an extreme example of how necessary it was to get myself in the right mood to hit my first tee shot. Remember, this was four-ball so it was a game for attack-ing, not playing safe.

The opening hole was a tough, tree-lined par four from an elevated tee. I remember feeling what I call 'happy excited' because I had been using all the tech-niques I had learned from Dr. John to get in the right mood to execute this vital shot as well as possible.

I must be honest and say I was feeling in complete awe of Woods and Duval, which wasn't particularly helpful. But I knew that I had to pay attention to what I was doing not on other people. I'm sure you can understand what it was like for me to be at arms' length from the most famous person in the world and probably the greatest golfer who has ever lived. So here I was chatting to him, waiting for our turn to play. I had to pinch myself to bring me back to earth because if I was going to spend the after-noon watching Tiger I probably wouldn't play very well. Don't forget I was representing my country too so I didn't want to let anyone down, including my partner Andrew.

So I looked down towards the grass on the tee and though I didn't close my eyes I took a mental journey a few thousand miles away from that tee, and Tiger and the pressure and the TV cameras and the thousands of fans. I took a journey like I did so successfully at Lundin Links just a couple of months before to qualify for the Open at St Andrews. I had to calm myself so I imagined I was back home in Scotland walking into my parents' house in Paisley, near Glasgow. I was walking through the front door and into the living room, visualising the glass sliding doors and feeling the carpet beneath my feet. I could see the couch I'd sat on so many times and the cabinet alongside the TV full of ornaments. I'm into the back room now and my mum and dad are there, smiling, comforting me. So all the anxiety has gone. I'm in my favourite place with my favourite people - a perfect environment where I feel at peace and comfortable. So I'm not nervous any more. I'm in a perfect state to play my shot.

It's my turn to play now. Some guy shouts my name over a loud speaker and I'm ready, slipping into my routine comfortably, focusing on the target, pulling the trigger and hitting the shot.

I remember hitting a great drive that actually went too far - the strike was so good the ball ran into a bunker. From there I had a long bunker shot but I continued using all the same techniques and they enabled me to flush a long iron to about 15 feet. That settled me and I went on to play really well despite all the hullabaloo. Heaven knows what would have happened if I hadn't had the relaxation techniques to get me in the right mood.

I started with five pars, nothing startling but steady and consistent. Then I birdied six holes on the row, which was an amazing experience that I'll tell you about in another chapter.

Andrew played great too and we shot a ten-under-par 62. I played well and the main reason was I knew how to relax myself.

How to Get in the Right Mood to Play your Best Golf

Dr. John

We have already discussed how to boost your confidence. You can use similar techniques to get yourself in the perfect mental state to play the best golf of your life. There is one simple sentence I want you to remember - positive emotions will lead to a better performance. And the opposite is true - negative emotions will destroy your performance.

Temper is a negative emotion. Thinking of hazards such as out-of-bounds, rivers and bunkers is another. Negative thinking causes stress, fear and anxiety, which are the major sources of problems for golfers. There are many unpleasant places your golf ball can end up - and they all frighten us. And if you constantly focus on these negative images you will end up with a phobia about a particular kind of shot.

I'm sure you've all heard of the yips, when you can't hole a tiny putt. That's a classic golfing phobia that affects many players. It's interesting that no one has ever had the yips on a 20-foot putt - the yips only seem to affect us on very short putts and that's because we expect to hole them.

After missing a few short putts, golfers begin to fear them. Unpleasant thoughts start to circulate inside their minds. You probably won't be consciously aware of it, but if you are suffering from the yips you are using imagery skills to contemplate how awful it would be to miss the putt. It would embarrass you and produce feelings of guilt, strong emotions that sap your confidence.

Focusing on these negative feelings amplifies them. These feelings get stronger and stronger and thinking this way has a particularly debilitating affect on sportsmen and women who are trying to accomplish precise actions that require fine movements.

So focusing on failure will not assist the performance of, say, a weightlifter or a prizefighter but it is unlikely to terminally affect his ability in the way such thoughts can destroy a snooker player, a darts player or a professional golfer.

Chipping and putting requires fine, precise movements when success or failure is measured in millimetres rather than metres. It will start with nerves - you will develop butterflies in your stomach and you'll start to cramp up and feel tense. That's what fear will do to you if you think you might fall off a cliff, if you are being driven too quickly in a fast motor car or if you are trying to hole a three-foot putt to win the Open Championship. Our minds have been programmed to work that way over thousands of years.

Fear creates a negative climate. Your thoughts affect your feelings and your feelings affect your behaviour. Then you're finished and on your way to another bad round, and the cycle begins all over again, on the range or the next time you play.

Psychologists call this classical conditioning. It's how we have evolved to learn. There are fundamental models of learning. We can learn by through association and by being patient. So if you associate your golf with negative emotional states such as stress and fear, that is exactly what will happen when you play. That will be part of your internal environment and you will stop enjoying the game and eventually, depending on your personality, you will probably lose heart, give up and end up mentally burnt out. It won't be fun any more. That's the most common reason why so many outstanding youngsters fail to fulfil their expectations – it's all because they started getting anxious and began swamping themselves by fear responses.

There is only one way out of this mess - you must teach yourself to focus on positive emotions, that is to say all the feelings you have when you are 'in the zone.' That means fun, excitement and confidence. You need a strategy that will get you in these states whenever you want.

Most of us play our best golf when we are relaxed. So you need to introduce a relaxation technique into your pre-shot routine. One trick that has worked very well for my Tour players is external imagery - using the power of your mind to see yourself from outside your body, as if you are looking at yourself on a television screen. This instantaneously detaches you from the emotion of the situation - remember it is negative feelings that destroy you. Tests have proved that if you can think this way, you won't have any feelings, either positive or negative. You'll be totally detached and neutral and this will stop negative feelings and manufacture confidence. This is also called a disassociative state.

So as you are walking towards the first tee, imagine looking down on yourself, see the clothes you are wearing, look at the colours and the playing partners who will be standing close to you. If you can make the imaginary television screen inside your head real, all your negative emotions will float away. They'll disappear. You'll be confident.

In another chapter we will talk about the benefits of a post-shot routine. You can use that here. There's plenty of time on your hands when you walk off the green or along the fairway. You can use some of this time wisely by thinking the right thoughts. You will need to concentrate intensely to make the images real and powerful. I'm not saying it will be easy but I am saying the effort will be worthwhile.

Another technique you can use is concentrating on a feeling which is the opposite of fear. Recall a time in your life when you have been courageous or when you have overcome adversity on the course and got the job done. You can also think of aggression.

When you feel stress there are two ways to respond. They are called the 'flight and fight response.' Broadly speaking you can either run away from whatever it is you feel threatened by or you can attack it. It's easier to understand this concept if you slip back in time a few thousand years, when our brains were evolving and imagine a stone age hunter being faced with a wild boar – attack or run away – get the picture?

We have evolved that way. Switching back to the golf course, aggression might help you. It can be a very positive emotion but aggression has to be controlled. If you are overly aggressive you will be too high and likely to play bad shots and make rash decisions. Your course management will be irresponsible. You will overestimate your abilities and attack the course too much.

You have to analyse what mood you are in when you play your best golf. There are patterns but we are all individuals. It's obvious that Colin Montgomerie needs to be relaxed. The big man needs to feel whimsical and in a fun mood.

Look at his record in the Ryder Cup and how he played at The Belfry in 2002. You might recall the last day when Europe held a narrow lead and Monty was the first player on the practise area where there were thousands of fans watching. The incident was broadcast live on Sky TV. Monty was in a spectacularly good mood. He was joking with the crowd as though he didn't have a care in the world. He even invited some guy from the stand to have a go at hitting his sand iron. The guy duffed it three times but when he finally hit a reasonable shot, the crowd went wild. The positive support for Monty was so powerful you could almost reach out and touch it. Monty fed off all this adulation and clicked into the perfect frame of mind for him to play the best golf of his life.

Monty went on and destroyed Scott Hoch in his singles match. I think Monty was six or seven under when the game was over on the 14th green. And Hoch was no pushover. He had played 24 consecutive years on the American Tour, piling up 17 victories and more than £12 million in prize money. Yet Monty humiliated him. And all because he was in the right mood to play golf.

For Monty there is something magical and inspirational about the Ryder Cup. Perhaps it's the togetherness of a team united with a common purpose - to beat the Americans. There's no doubt that if Monty could reproduce his mental state on the final day at The Belfry, he would win more tournaments. I still think he's capable of winning Majors now. He has all the ability, all he needs to do is figure out a way to relax and have more fun when he is playing.

Ian Poulter provides another example of how a change of mood on the golf course can produce massive benefits. In 2003 he struggled in the first part of the season, missing four cuts in the first five tournaments. That's not like him. Ian is a terrific player who has huge self belief. Then he won the Welsh Open at Celtic Manor, with an incredible 18-under-par total earning more than £200,000. Everyone knew how good Ian was but that superb performance had not been expected. Ian followed that win with a host of wonderful displays and more victories, eventually finishing fifth in the European Tour Order of Merit, earning more than £1 million. I've spoken to Ian about his dramatic change of form. He told me he plays his best when he feels happy. Ian had somehow figured out a way to do that at Celtic Manor, and kept it going for the rest of the season.

I started working with Ryder Cup player Paul Broadhurst last year and we soon figured out that his emotional keys to playing well were relaxation and fun. We worked on that really hard before he played at Gleneagles in the Diageo Championship. Paul finished third on six-under for the tournament, just three behind Søren Kjeldsen. He earned more than £70,000 in his best finish on the Tour for some time. That's how powerful thinking the right way can be for Tour players. You can gain the same benefits.

Tour players are awesome at playing golf. Even though I have attended dozens of tournaments and watched the greatest players in the world many times, their talent never stops amazing me. When they play with their pals in a relaxed situation they usually shoot eight-

or-nine under par - and that's all of them - even some unknown guy from Korea or Japan who you have never heard of. But they usually don't play as well in the tournament. Only the true champions do that. That's because in a practise round they are relaxed. It's fun. But add the pressure of a big championship, a few million pounds in prize money and crowds of 30,000 and they start to feel different. There's too much pressure and tension.

So most Tour players are like you. Their brains work exactly the same way. You need to use the techniques we have talked about to replace fear with confidence.

If you feel more comfortable playing with your friends, use your mind to imagine they are there, with you. Picture them talking to you and congratulating you on a particularly good drive or an accurate iron shot. You can think this way before your shots and walking between your shots. Or you can begin to bombard yourself with positive images of playing good golf while you are driving to the course. It's all about a change of attitude. Find out the most powerful image that will relax you. The most common one for Tour players are images of their families. For you it might be your friends, your wife or your girlfriend, going to the cinema, even a football match, perhaps music. Think about it. Work out the people and places where you feel most comfortable and happy.

Believe it or not, some of the younger European Tour players flirt with pretty girls on the course, actually during a tournament. I'm sure that will surprise you but when the girls smile back, it makes the players feel confident and special, they enjoy the experience and all of a sudden the bogey on the previous hole might not seem important. They are having fun again. They're relaxed and confident. The world's greatest players can create positive thoughts whenever they want using all the techniques we have talked about. So can you.

Summary

A positive mental state will allow you to play your best golf. Get rid of those negative thoughts and figure out the emotions that will allow you to play your best golf. For most of us, that will be a combination of fun, confidence and relaxation. Focus on these thoughts before you play, immerse yourself in them using some of the techniques we have talked about. This kind of thinking can be part of your pre-shot and post-shot routine. All these emotions are associated with your best swing. If you can do that you will be capable of playing the best golf of your life.

CHAPTER SIX

Pre-Shot and
Post-Shot Routines

Dean

A pre-shot routine is important because it will help to get you into the correct emotional state. You want to control your emotions and prevent them from going up or down.

I can remember the final round of the PGA Championships at Wentworth in 1998 when I was playing with Colin Montgomerie and I had an opportunity to win the tournament and change my life for ever. I was in the zone perfectly. Everything was so easy. I was feeling lots of positive emotions and this was helping me to keep hitting good shots and holing important putts. Then one wrong thought changed everything. All of a sudden I was in an uncomfortable environment and I didn't like it. I struggled badly on the last four holes and it was all due to the negative emotions I was feeling.

Of course, I didn't know what to do back then so I couldn't change what was hurting me. I could handle the situation much better now. Most of us know the importance of a pre-shot routine but a post-shot routine can be just as vital yet hardly anyone uses this technique.

If you hit a great shot, say a drive right down the middle of the fairway, or a short iron six feet from the pin, you'll feel a high. And if you hit a poor shot, duff a long iron or miss a short putt, you'll feel low. That's the way your mind works and it's likely to have a major effect on your next shot.

A post-shot routine can virtually guarantee that you'll be in the right mental state to perform at your peak. If you are too high you should think about using relaxation techniques to calm you down. After hitting a great shot you must take care to control your excitement, to bring yourself down from the high. We've all seen boxers who have won important championships conducting incoherent interviews when they are overcome with emotion, moments after the final bell. So imagine such a boxer being asked to perform a feat of precise concentration such as holing a downhill right-to-left six-foot putt to make a cut or win a tournament. Do you think he would hole it? Probably not.

And if you've played a poor shot the opposite is the case. You'll be down and disappointed and you'll need to boost your confidence and the easiest way to do this is to access great shots you've hit before.

I'll tell you an extreme story of another amazing round I had at Wentworth. It was the PGA championships again, this time in 1997. Wentworth is one of my favourite golf courses I was really keyed up to play well. I stood on the first tee in the first round feeling really pumped up. I hit a great drive down the left hand side of the fairway and even now, after all these years, I can still remember the exact yardage to the pin – 198 yards. My caddy and I selected a five iron and I hit the perfect shot, drawing in to the green – two bounces and straight in the hole for a two.

I gave my caddy a high five that nearly knocked him out and as we walked onto the green the crowd were going bananas. So you can imagine the state my mind was in. I've played one hole and I'm two-under yet I've still got another 71 holes to go.

So I'm standing on the second hole, which is a tricky, short par three and I'm so high yet I don't know how to get myself down. I hit a seven-iron and I flushed it and the ball's right on the pin all the way. The problem was it was two clubs too big because I was so pumped up. We watched the crowd behind the green dispersing and shouting 'fore' before getting out of the way. The ball bounces once before diving into the trees so I'd hit a perfect shot way too big because of all the adrenaline. I managed a five for an eagle, double-bogey start when it would have been better to have had two straight pars. That way my mind would have been calm and controlled, instead of all those extreme emotions messing it up.

Somehow I managed to par the third but my amazing round had another twist on the fourth, a par five where I was just short of the green in two. So I'm faced with this incredibly tough chip, right to left, over a ridge. I hit a good shot with a lob wedge and I knew right away it was going to be pretty close. On and on it rolled, taking the break perfectly, before dropping in for another eagle. So I'm up again, as high as a kite as I walked onto the fifth, another par three.

OK, I said to myself, don't make the same mistake you did on the second. I hit a six iron instead of a five to compensate for my high mental state and the ball finished close to the pin for an easy two. What a start – eagle, double bogey, par, eagle, birdie, and I'm three under. If I remember correctly I had another eagle on the 12th and another double bogey on the way to a level-par 72.

I'd played some of the best golf of my life but because I was unable to control my emotions I'd blown a good score. I was gutted. When I walked off the 18th tee I was drained, as if I had just run a marathon. I was emotionally bashed.

My problems all started on the second tee after my eagle two at the first. I should have relaxed my muscles and taken a few deep breaths before using one of my favourite techniques, which is going on a journey away from what is making me think so inefficiently.

If I'm too high I like to go to a particular beach in the Caribbean where I enjoyed a great holiday a few years ago. I would let the feelings consume me, making the journey seem real so that I could almost bend down and run my hands through the soft, golden sand and sense the cool water washing over my feet. I'd see the beautiful blue sky, hear the seabirds overhead and feel that glorious sun burning my face.

Of course, it's a touch easier for a European Tour player who works closely with someone like Dr. John. We have a programme worked out using particular mental techniques for specific situations. My journey to the Caribbean wasn't a spur of the moment decision. We had worked this journey out together, knowing that this mental trick would be likely to work for me in certain situations. You can do that too.

We have a range of good feelings to draw on. It's like going to a shop or a library to take out a book. What you need is your own library, with your own thoughts to draw on that are specific to you.

A common theme among Tour players is families. That's where many of us feel comfortable - with our parents, brothers and sisters or wives and children. Perhaps that might not be successful for you. You have to figure out what works best. Find out where you feel most comfortable and use those feelings before and after your shot. The answers are all there in your mind. It's just a case of working them out.

Why Every Champion has a Pre-Shot and Post-Shot Routine

Dr. John

You might not know it, but you already have a pre-shot and post-shot routine. But they almost certainly need improving. Before you hit the ball you will be thinking of something. Most golfers think a pre-shot routine means one specific gimmick which kick-starts their swing. It could be a waggle, a turn of the head or a distinct movement such as kicking in your knee or pressing your toes together. These thoughts might have moderate benefits if they control your concentration but there's so much more you can do to improve your play.

The purpose of a pre-shot routine should be to get yourself into the right mental state. How many of you do that? Hardly anyone, I bet. I'm not suggesting you should ignore the technical fundamentals of a good swing – a sound grip and correct alignment to the target. What I am saying is that most of us attempt to aim towards the target when it is probably more important to get in the right mood.

A good mental pre-shot routine will assist you to get 'in the zone.' Imagine your zone is a piece of cake. Your zone is characterised by a number of ingredients such as feelings and emotions. We are all different. Some players need to feel aggressive to play their best golf, while others prefer to be relaxed and more emotionally stable.

To try to help you understand the practicalities of my teaching I'm going to tell you about a pre-shot and post routine that helped Darren Clarke win the English Open a couple of years ago. We've talked about this before but the big man's experiences will give you a perfect example of the benefits of thinking correctly, of getting into your zone.

Darren had a terrible round in the Pro-Am the day before the actual tournament. He had fallen into the habit of using his pre-shot routine to focus on bad shots, technique and outcomes – the result was catastrophic – he shot 84. I talked with Darren that evening and we worked out a different way of thinking designed to help him get in his zone. He started relaxing, and began to focus on getting into a high, emotional state by recalling how he felt when he played his best. The next day he shot 65, a reduction of 19 shots. It takes some believing, doesn't it?

He went on to win the tournament with a 17-under-par total. We talked for a while after the prize giving and Darren told me that the only time he stopped thinking correctly was on the 17th tee in the final round, when the pressure was at its highest. He hit a poor tee shot into deep rough and he was forced to hack the ball back onto the fairway. The lie was terrible and he had no alternative. His bad tee-shot was a wake-up call so Darren slipped comfortably back into the correct way of thinking, returned into his zone immediately and hit a perfect eight-iron that finished a metre from the flag. He went on to par the 18th and win his first title for almost a year – and all because he used his mind to think the right way before and after every shot.

Summary

Your pre-shot and post-shot routines should incorporate mental skills that get you into the right feelings and emotions that will make it more likely for you to get 'in your zone.' If you go out on the golf course and think the right way, you will find your zone most of the time.

You will have read plenty of articles which refer to goal-setting but they usually involve a measurable improvement in your game such as shooting a certain score or reducing your handicap. I recommend that you stop thinking this way and make your goal to 'enter your zone' whenever you play. The difference will be amazing.

That's the mental attitude you need to play your best golf. If you aren't looking for your zone you will never find it and you will have no chance of fulfilling your potential.

Chapter Seven

How to Control your Temper

Dean

If you lose your temper, you're finished on the golf course. A lot of things will start to happen in your mind and they're all bad. You will probably play too quickly, lose control, possibly give up, get down on yourself, get too tense and lose concentration. That's a long list of things you don't want to happen when it matters most.

I've always been pretty good at controlling my temper on the golf course, in fact, staying cool is one of my biggest attributes. But I remember losing my temper big style and playing very badly because of it in the Victor Chandler British Masters at Woburn Golf Club in 2001. I finished up frustrated, embarrassed and at least £10,000 out of pocket and all because I failed to control my temper.

I was playing really well and began the tournament with a level-par 72 followed by two 70s to put me on four-under going into the final round. To be honest I wasn't happy with my score. Everything about my game was perfect but I just couldn't hole any putts. You get days like that sometimes on the Tour and normally I would be patient and wait for them to drop. Not this time though.

I'd had loads of opportunities and every time I missed a birdie putt I could feel myself getting more and more frustrated.

I sensed the anger building up inside me after I missed another putt on the par five 11th and though I knew that sort of thinking would hurt me, I didn't know how to stop. I walked off the green, shaking my head, and slammed the putter into the bag. It gets worse because then I decided to kick the bag after I rammed the putter in.

The next hole was a short par four, just 343 yards. The big boys can drive the green so it was one of the easiest holes on the course and an obvious birdie opportunity. I hit quite a good drive into a greenside bunker, followed by a decent splash shot to about six feet. My caddie Brian took my sand iron and handed me the putter. We just stared at each other without saying a word – I'd damaged the club kicking my bag on the previous hole and now it had loads of loft on it. The club looked more like a seven iron. I'd bent the hosel and the putter was too damaged to use. It didn't make any difference anyway because the Rules of Golf state you can't use equipment that has been altered on the course.

So here I am, heading for a good finish and a big cheque in an important tournament on slick greens, which are as quick as a snooker table - and I haven't got a putter. And all because I've lost my temper.

Over the last seven holes I tried putting with loads of different clubs - sand wedges, wedges, a nine iron and my five iron. Nothing worked and I shot seven over for the last seven holes. I'd thrown shots away like confetti. I finished bogey, bogey, double bogey, bogey, par, bogey, bogey.

After three rounds I was sitting nicely in 16th position at four-under and playing well. When I'd lost my cool on the 11th I was five-under-par for the tournament and looking for a solid finish and a nice cheque. But I lost my cool and shot a horrible 77. It still hurts now thinking about it. So losing my temper had plummeted me from the top ten to 53rd and a £4,000 cheque. If I'd just parred the remaining holes for a 71 I would have finished 15th and picked up £17,000. The eventual winner was Frenchman Thomas Levet who sneaked a play-off against English-man David Howell and Swedish pair Robert Karlsson and Mathias Gronberg.

Of course, it's not all about scores and money. Losing my temper and kicking my bag made me look stupid in front of the gallery. I was embarrassed. Golf fans are not used to seeing Tour players using wedges to putt with on pristine greens.

The whole incident was upsetting and costly in every way so I have a clear memory of how destructive losing your temper can be.

There are plenty of players in world golf who struggle to control their temper on the course. Zimbabwean Tony Johnstone comes to mind and then there's Masters cham-pion Craig Stadler. Another American, Paul Azinger, snapped his putter in half live in front of the television cameras in the 1999 US Open that Payne Stewart went on to win with a spectacular 15-foot par putt on the 18th at Pinehurst.

You may recall Ben Crenshaw in the 1987 Ryder Cup at Muirfield Village in Ohio, when Jack Nicklaus became the first American captain to lose the cup in the States. Irishman Eamonn Darcy was drawn to play Ben in the final day singles. Ben was officially the best putter in the world so everyone was predicting a comfortable win for the Americans. But Ben missed a short putt on the sixth green, lost his cool and broke his putter across his knee. Eamonn was three up at the turn but Ben fought back and was one up with two to play, despite using a 1-iron or his sand wedge to putt with. Eamonn showed great courage to win the last two holes and the Ryder Cup was heading back across the Atlantic. Many of you will remember Jose-Maria Olazabal doing the cha-cha on the 18th green while the Americans looked on gloomily. The final result was 15-13 to the Europeans. If Ben had not lost his temper the United States might have won the Ryder Cup.

So regardless of how frustrated you are, you must control your temper.

How to Control your Temper

Dr. John

I have huge admiration for Colin Montgomerie. He is a
great champion and his feat of winning seven consecutive
European Tour Orders of Merit will probably never be
beaten. But Monty is a classic example of how destructive it can be to lose your temper on the golf course. As
soon as he starts losing his cool in a tournament, a bogey
will follow - you can guarantee it. And usually he follows
it with another and another and the next thing you know,
he's bombing out of the tournament. Monty could have
won a lot more events if he had been able to control his
temper. He admits that in his autobiography.

Darren Clarke is another player who has lost tournaments through his inability to control his temper. That's
how he threw away the 2003 Masters. It was the same
story as Monty, that same predictable cycle - a bit of bad
luck, lost temper - bogey, bogey, bogey.

Darren was winning the Masters after a first round
66. He had played superbly, shooting five birdies, an
eagle and just one bogey. Everyone was tipping him to
carry on the good form and win his first Major. But on
the second day he bogeyed the first on his way to a 76 in
a roller-coaster round that included six bogeys and one
double bogey. Then he shot 78, in a mediocre round that

included four bogeys and a horrendous nine. In the final round, Darren played pretty well but his 74 left him well down the field, 13 shots behind Canadian Mike Weir, who won after a play-off.

I was working with Darren when he played in the Volvo Masters at Valderrama, a couple of years ago. He is a wonderfully talented golfer and after a steady opening score he was putting together a fabulous second round and closing in on the leaders. Then things got even better. Darren hit a spectacular hole in one on the 15th to go seven-under par. But on the 17th he ran up a double bogey. I knew what was going to happen - he followed that with another double on the last - so four shots had gone in just two holes and all because he could not snap out of the mental state he was in after the 17th. He went on to finish in the top 10 but he probably should have won the tournament. He was playing well enough. Darren failed primarily because of the last two holes in the second round, when he couldn't control his temper. You may recall Monty and Bernhard Langer shared the title after darkness prevented the play-off continuing.

Last year I started working with the German player Tobias Dier. He has stacks of talent and I think he might become a really great player. But like Monty and Darren, he can lose his temper on the golf course. He told me one of the biggest regrets of his career was when he threw away the Mauritius Open.

The 18th hole at Belle Mare Plage Links is a tough par five requiring a long tee shot where most of the pros use drivers to cut the ball around a dog-leg with water on the right. Tobias was in the lead on the last hole in the last round. He hit a great tee shot but he thought his line was a touch too far right. Tobias convinced himself that his ball was out-of-bounds. He got so mad that he smashed his driver into his bag and broke it in half. When he got down the fairway his drive was perfect but he was still thinking of his broken driver, and struggled to concentrate, having to settle for a par when a birdie would have won him the tournament. But at least he had made the play-offs. The trouble was the first play-off hole was the 18th - and guess what, Tobias didn't have his driver. So he lost to a birdie and the tournament he should have won was snatched from him because he lost his temper.

Another guy I work with on Tour is Chris Gane. Most of you won't have heard of him, but Chris has a sensational short game - as good as anyone on Tour. He's a fantastic pitcher and putter. But he gets angry with himself too often and that hurts him really badly. Temper plagues his game and he turns into a mediocre player. That creates a negative emotion, which is so powerful he starts thinking of bad swings and the next thing you know he's hitting bad shots and shooting 75s.

So now you know that Tour players are the same as the rest of us. Most of them struggle to control their temper when things go wrong. The answer for them and you is to regain emotional control, which means controlling your thoughts, your feelings, and your behaviour. One way is through imagery - that can be your saviour.

Let's take a look at what Tobias should have done on the 18th tee at Mauritius. He thought he had blown the tournament so in an instant he was bombarding himself with negative feelings - a moment later the red mist came down and he had lost his temper and started behaving irrationally. That's when he smashed his bag and broke his driver.

What he should have done is use imagery to see the most perfect shot he could have hit in a theoretical television screen inside his head. As he was walking off the tee, down the fairway, Tobias should have pictured a great swing he had hit earlier that day or that season - perhaps he might have visualised a drive Ernie Els or Tiger Woods had hit in similar circumstances. Tobia's mind would have allowed him to change reality so instead of a gloomy walk down the fairway thinking his ball was in the water, he could have been feeling wonderful, the way he would have been if he had hit the right shot.

You can do this with any shot you're not happy with. It really works. Your mind can make your subconscious think that you have actually hit a great shot or holed a long putt and your brain will be flooded with positive feelings and you will soak up all the benefits they bring, such as relaxation, confidence and fun. Then it won't even cross your mind to throw your clubs – you'll be on a high.

The reason we lose our temper is often embarrassment. We think bad play is an ego threat. You will react to adversity differently if you look on a bad shot as a challenge. If your ball is in a bunker, think how great you will feel if you get up and down - or even hole it. That kind of thinking will take the pressure off.

The true champions are usually the best scramblers in the world, not the best drivers. There are better drivers and iron players than Tiger Woods. The statistics prove that. But he beats them all because when he misses a green he nearly always gets up and down.

Look at Severiano Ballesteros - three Opens, two Masters, more than 80 Tour victories worldwide and he's all over the place from the tee. Seve's short game is still magical. Where do you think Seve would be if he had lost his temper every time he missed a fairway or green? Nowhere. In his prime, Seve was a positive player who assumed if he missed a green he would hole his next shot. You should think that way too.

Summary

If you can feel yourself losing your temper because you've hit a bad shot, look away and visualise the perfect shot you had hoped to hit. So if you have sliced your ball out of bounds, replay the shot inside you head and see the ball soaring into the distance, splitting the fairway.

Secondly, wherever your ball has gone, think of your next shot as a challenge. Get into this new way of thinking. Say to yourself: "I'm going to hole my next shot," that's the way children think. So start thinking like a child who hasn't matured enough to understand the pressures you are under or how important golf is to you.

If a bad shot has put you in a difficult position, look at it as an opportunity, not a disaster. You can impress your friends or playing partners with how good you are at scrambling. Start reframing your world like this and you will be more positive and begin to enjoy your golf more. A merry-go-round ride is boring. It's more fun on the roller-coaster. A round of golf is like that, full of highs and lows - enjoy the highs, the great shots, and look at the lows, and the bad shots with excitement. If you can do that you will make a dramatic improvement in your scores.

CHAPTER EIGHT

Why do you Play Great on The Range and Terrible on the Course?

Dean

Most of the time you feel relaxed on the driving range, much more than you do on the course, especially in an important competition. You let go, you are less careful and you commit yourself fully to your shots. The environment on the range is comfortable and most of the time you will strike your shots with good rhythm. There is less interference.

The explanation is obvious. There's no-one watching, there's nothing at stake and there's no out-of-bounds, tall trees or rivers or bunkers. If you hit a bad shot, so what? You haven't got a card in your hand. On the range every shot is straightforward. It's just a matter of picking your target and away you go. That's why, generally, most of us hit better shots on the range, than we do on the course.

On the course, most of the time, you think completely differently than you do on the range. And the main difference is mental interference. We allow other things to invade our minds and spoil our concentration. All the thoughts that are absent on the range come flooding into your mind, without warning, and you probably won't be able to stop them. It might be the wind, hazards, out-of-bounds, people watching, high rough, narrow fairways or tight pins. There's a stack of thoughts that infiltrate your mind and hurt your ability to play freely.

The shot itself will be exactly the same, what's different is how your mind perceives the situation. The golf ball doesn't know where the pin is or how difficult the shot might be or who is watching.

On the range, a golf professional would think nothing of hitting a drive to an imaginary fairway no wider than 10 yards. Most of the time he would make that shot successfully but put him in a different environment and it's often another story. Now imagine the pro is faced with a tee-shot on the sixth hole at Carnoustie in the final round of the Open Championship. That's a tough shot for anyone. You won't get a more difficult tee shot than the sixth at Carnoustie anywhere. The hole is a 578-yard par five with out-of-bounds all the way along the left-hand side of the fairway but you can't bale out to the right because in an Open Championship the rough will be like a hay field. So you are forced to take on the shot and try to hit the fairway which seems as narrow as a small country road, the gap reducing even more by the presence of two horrible bunkers just 20 yards in from the out-of-bounds. Let's add a strong wind from the right, blowing your ball towards those white posts that frighten all golfers. Oh, and don't forget about the television cameras and a couple of thousand fans. Then there's all that pressure piling down on top of you. It's easy to see why, all of sudden, your mind starts to think in a completely different way.

On the range, you wouldn't concern yourself about the out-of-bounds or the bunkers. All you would do is pick a target and generally that's where the ball would go. But in the tournament or in your club medal, it's tough to prevent your mind focusing on other things such as crowds, titles, bunkers and getting your handicap down. That makes you tight and super careful. Negative thinking will destroy you and make it impossible to concentrate correctly.

One famous hole in golf which illustrates this perfectly is the 17th at Sawgrass where the Tournament Players' Championship is played in the United States every year. The hole is a short par three, only 132 yards, no more than a wedge or a smooth nine iron in calm conditions - a straightforward, simple shot for any competent player.

On the range a tournament professional's success rate on a hole like this would be very high. I would say he would expect to hit the green 17 or 18 times out of 20 and he would be miffed if he didn't hit the shot pretty close. Of course there's one thing missing on the range. Water.

The 17th is an island green surrounded by water. On the tee all you can see is water and a small green. That's how your mind will see the shot if you don't know how to control the way you think. There's no bale out anywhere - so you are either putting or you're in the water looking at a double bogey or worse- there's no other option. Yet the shot is exactly the same as on the range, a smooth nine-iron. What could be easier?

Back in 1997, Len Mattiace came to the 17th tee at Sawgrass with a chance of winning the Tournament Players' Championship. He was on top of his game, hitting great shots and holing lots of putts and he just had two holes to go. Then he started to see the water. Len concentrated on the water instead of the target and 10 minutes later he was walking off the green with a horrendous 8, after knocking his tee shot in the water twice. And don't go thinking Len is a rookie who couldn't cut it. He's won a few tournaments and more than £4m on the US Tour so his spectacular failure illustrates what can happen to you when you think the wrong way. You have to learn to think the way you do on the range when you are on the course.

The shot was identical. What's different is how Len began to think when he saw the water. OK, this is a particularly extreme example that plays havoc with the best players in the world every year. Without the water the hole is easy. The water changes your perception but the shot is still exactly the same - a smooth nine iron. So take it away. Ignore it. Your mind can do that.

We've all been in a similar situation on our own course when we are confronted by a tough shot that is important. It might be a tight drive or a difficult par three surrounded by bunkers. Suddenly you will feel tense, anxious and nervous. You will be acutely aware of all the negatives, and thinking like this will make a successful shot impossible. But there is a solution. You must use your mind to go back to the range using some of the techniques we have already talked about.

Relax yourself, focus on the target, get in the right mood to play the best shot of your life, go through your pre-shot routine and don't think about technique.

Not many of you will get the chance to play the 17th at Sawgrass. But certain holes can produce the same feelings. This will affect your mind in the exactly the same as the water at the 17th at Sawgrass affected Len Mattiace. That's why Justin Leonard won the title.

Dr. John will teach you how you can take the game you have on the range or the practise putting green out on to the course. He will show you how to pretend you are on the range and how you can change the water into grass in your mind. So now the water isn't there and you are left with a simple shot and all you have to do us focus on the target and hit the ball – just like you do on the range, time and time again.

I know one thing for sure – Dr. John's techniques work for me and they will work for you too.

Why do you Play Great on the Range and Terrible on The Course?

Dr. John

I've worked with plenty of players of all abilities who can hit the ball awesome on the range, but put them on the course, with a card in their hand and they go to pieces. This is a common fault among golfers. Usually it affects players who need to feel relaxed to get into their zone, and play good golf.

There is a scientific explanation. On the course, the environment is different and there is usually something at stake, from wanting to perform well in a tournament to playing with your pals for a few drinks or a couple of pounds. This kind of thinking makes most players excited, anxious and nervous. That kind of mental state can destroy you.

On the range we feel comfortable. The range is a trigger that allows us to feel relaxed. We associate the range with fun and though no one enjoys an unsatisfactory session when our ball striking is mediocre, it really doesn't matter. No one is watching and nothing is at stake. Now go to the first tee on the course and imagine how you will feel in an important tournament with 20 or 30 people watching you out of the club house window and that out-of-bounds fence or lake eating away at your confidence. The difference is obvious.

If you ever get the chance to attend a Tour event, try to take time to visit the practise area and watch these wonderful players hitting the ball. Believe me, you will not be able to separate the champion from the also-ran, struggling to keep his Tour card. They all hit the ball so effortlessly and with such wonderful rhythm, you wonder how any of these players could ever bogey a hole. They're that good.

I could get Tiger Woods to hit balls alongside, say, the 100th best player on the European Tour and they would more or less strike their shots the same. I know it takes some believing but I'm telling you the truth. I see it every week. They are professional players and this is what they have dedicated their lives to for more than 20 years.

But if they go on to the golf course, their emotions change. Tiger Woods can control his feelings through the power of his mind. All champions can do that, so while Woods is shooting low scores and piling up Major championships, the also-rans freeze, get nervous and miss cuts. It has more to do with their minds than how far or straight they hit their drivers.

When I began working with a certain Tour player last year, we met on the range while he was warming up for a tournament. I don't want to tell you his name but I will tell you he is a fantastic player.

I watched him hitting balls and I was taken aback by his ability and the effortless style he used to blast the ball. He told me that he usually struggles to take that form onto the course - nerves get in his way. But on the range, well, he hits the ball as good as any champion. He can do things with a golf ball on the range that you won't believe – high shots, low shots, soft fades, big slices, massive hooks – he can do anything. But on the golf course, sadly, his performance is dramatically different. We are making progress now and I am confident he'll win a tournament soon. Lots of Tour players are like that.

These players are permitting their environment to control their emotions. It doesn't have to be that way. Your internal environment is entirely down to you. You can see the world any way you want by using the power of your mind. If you associate a competition with stress, that's what you'll get, and if the prime emotion you feel on the course is anxiety, you won't be relaxed and you'll get nervous. It is impossible to play well like that.

So change it. If you see a competition as a relaxing challenge where you will have fun, that's what you'll get. I guarantee it. Is the glass half full or half empty? You do have a choice. Again, I'm not saying it will be easy. You'll have to practise thinking positively and I know how tough that can be – pessimism seems to be a way of thinking that many Britons drift into. We are a pessimistic nation.

I've travelled all over the world working with golf professionals and there is a difference in the way people from various countries interpret the world. Americans and Australians are incredibly optimistic. That's one of the reasons why those countries produce better sportsmen and women. They are not more skilled but they do have a different attitude. For them, sporting competition is a positive experience. And consequently Australians and Americans are refreshing people to be around. They are great examples to the rest of us. Start thinking like that and you won't just enjoy your golf more, you'll start getting more out of life.

Another obvious reason why most of us hit the ball well on the range and poorly on the course is the absence of outcomes. It doesn't matter if the ball goes left or right, in the lake or along the ground. All we're trying to do on the range is choose a target and get into a groove. There is no fear.

The trick is to think the same way on the course as you do on the range. Concentrate on your target and rhythm and you will be able to reproduce the same level of performance on the course as when you are relaxed and hitting good shots on the range. Problems occur when you focus on all the wrong thoughts such as hazards, how bad you will feel if you fail or what your final score will be. You can't play good golf thinking that way. It's impossible.

You can dictate your internal environment. How you feel doesn't have to be random. If you think correctly, you can be in the right relaxed 'driving range' state of mind when you play on the course, even in an important tournament.

We've talked in other chapters about using imagery to take a mental journey to a place where you feel comfortable. That will relax you, reduce those negative feelings and allow you to play well.

Graham McDowell, the Northern Ireland Tour player, who enjoyed a sensational amateur career, provides an inspiring example of this. In his first season on Tour, Graham was playing in the 2002 Scandinavian Masters at Kunsängen Golf Club in Stockholm. It was only his fourth event but Graham was playing great and leading the tournament with just four holes to go. Then he shanked the ball. I can't recall seeing a Tour player do that before. A shank at such a crucial point in the tournament would have destroyed other players who did not have the mental strength of Graham. They would have felt embarrassed and doubts and negative thoughts would have enveloped them. But not Graham.

He ignored it. In his mind it simply hadn't happened. Graham kept in the same frame of mind as if he was relaxing on the range, hitting balls alongside his pals. He used the mental tools that had helped him reach the top of the leaderboard.

Graham pulled himself together so efficiently he birdied the next hole despite some of the best players in the world breathing down his neck. He parred the final two holes to win the tournament and more than £200,000 on 14-under-par, one shot ahead of South African Trevor Immelman. You should start thinking the same way.

Summary

You need to create your own internal world and prevent the environment from changing the way you think. You hit the ball better on the range because you are relaxed, don't worry about where the ball is going to finish and never think about outcomes.

So train your mind to think exactly the same way on the course. Just like Graham McDowell. Then magical things will start to happen.

CHAPTER NINE

Hole More Putts
by Thinking Correctly

Dean

All the techniques I have already shared with you will help to improve your putting. The principles are the same - recalling great putts you have holed, getting in a positive frame of mind, forgetting about technique and relaxation. But there's one more trick I have up my sleeve that can make a big difference to how you perform on the greens. Psychologists call it centring but I'll tell you more about that later. Firstly I want to tell you about one of my best putting days and how I used my mind to help me shoot a stack of birdies.

I've already told you about when I played with Tiger Woods and David Duval in the 2001 World Cup at The Taiheiyo Club in Shizouka, Japan. Remember how I got into the right mood to hit a good tee shot off the first with thousands of people watching? Now I'll finish the story.

I was representing Scotland with Andrew Coltart, so you can imagine how important it was to put in a good performance. We were playing in the third round and the format was four-ball, which means you have to shoot for birdies all the time. I went on to par the first five holes and this steady start calmed me down nicely. The sixth is a tough, long par five and if you want to reach the putting surface in two, you have to hit a long approach over water, which surrounds the small green. I watched and admired Tiger hitting the best shot I'd seen in my life - a four iron close to the pin to set up an eagle chance. I still needed a three-wood, which I hit pretty well but it drifted into a greenside bunker. A good splash shot left me 10 feet from the hole and I was faced with a really tough downhill putt. I used all the techniques we have talked about - centring, physical relaxation and visualisation. I painted an imaginery orange line on the green and made the hole stand out vividly by brightening the white paint inside the cup. In my mind, it was easy for me to track the ball all the way to the hole, and that helped me to think positively. I hit a great putt to make birdie, so now I'm one-under for the round.

The next hole is a par three where I hit a good six iron to 15 feet. I can still remember the line - I read the putt to break a cup and half to the left. I used the same techniques and they were becoming more and more vivid and powerful. Already I was starting to think I couldn't miss, so I painted the same thin orange line on the green, which mirrored the way I sometimes practised, using an actual chalk line. Finally I imagined the white paint on the plastic below the cup standing out even more, making the colour the brightest white you can imagine. My ball dives in without touching the sides for another birdie.

On the eighth I had another long putt, this time around 30 feet, with a huge 15-foot left-to-right borrow.

The green is similar to the ninth at Augusta. I had a great feel for what the ball was going to do, almost as if I could see into the future; I sensed the contours perfectly and repeated the same process. I hit the putt exactly the way I wanted and away it went, round and round, on and on, until it fell into the hole. Three-under and I'm on a roll.

I hit a four-iron to the ninth, just a touch too hard, and the ball went to the back right of the green, resting on the fringe, 45 feet from the pin. I was faced with a horrendous putt, up a slope, then downhill with a massive right-to-left borrow. Another imaginary orange line appears on the green, and everything is looking good - I feel like I'm on remote control, my feel for the line and speed is instinctive, and all I'm doing is following the process without thinking too much, and in it goes for my fourth birdie.

On the tenth I was left with a 25-foot putt, over a slight crown then downhill all the way. My caddy Brian confirmed my feeling that the putt was perfectly straight and I just knew over the ball that I was going to make it. I went through my routine, relaxing and centring and hit a perfect putt like I knew I would, on the perfect line with the perfect weight. It couldn't miss. Now I've got five birdies in a row.

The 11th is a par five and I hit two powerful, straight shots just short of the green before I chipped up to around eight feet. In my mind, after holing all those tough breaking putts on the previous holes, it felt like a tap-in because I was thinking so well. This will sound strange but I knew it was in when I was marking the ball. It was a lightning fast downhill putt but missing didn't cross my mind, not for a moment. That's what thinking the right way can do for you. I was completely in my bubble of concentration.

As I picked the ball out of the hole and the crowd began to cheer, I could see Tiger laughing with my caddie Brian, as if he was saying: 'how can this guy putt so good?'

So I'd holed six tough putts under the severest of pressure, playing with the world's greatest player. I finally missed one on the 12th, and if memory serves, it was another long putt from the fringe of the green. I was actually shocked that it didn't go in. My line was perfect but I left it six inches short and I couldn't believe it. How could I miss?

The next hole was a long par-three and I hit a four-iron into a bunker. I splashed out to eight feet but my partner Andrew Coltart had already got the par. I remember Tiger's caddie Steve Williams picking my ball up and handing it to me. He was smiling, saying: 'I'll give you that. You can't miss today.'

You might like to know that Andrew and I shot 62, ten-under-par to be right up there among the leaders. Andrew played really great. We followed that up with a disappointing 71, but we had finished on 18-under, to come a creditable 11th in a field full of the world's greatest players. Ernie Els and Retief Goosen won the title for South Africa after winning a play-off against the Americans and the Danes.

Let's examine this technique called centring. Dr. John will go into more detail about this but here's a simple explanation about how it works for me. Firstly, you need to figure out your centre of gravity, which for most people is three fingers below the belly button. Then, as you are preparing to putt, take a deep breath and exhale, all the time focusing on that point, on your centre of gravity. That gets me feeling really balanced and relaxed. When I'm putting well, that's all I need to do. And if it's my day the putts drop. Somehow all the thoughts I need to concentrate on to enable me to putt well just happen. Centring keeps the lower half of my body perfectly still and stops me from thinking about technique or line. It gives me a great awareness for line and feel. There's a kind of correlation between my centre of gravity, the ball and the hole. It's tough to explain but hopefully you'll get the general picture and Dr. John will teach you how you can use this technique.

I'll try to explain how your mind can work against you if you don't know how to think correctly. If you try a 20-foot putt you might hole it, but there's a pretty good chance you'll miss it too. So the pressure isn't very high. Now make it three feet and add a touch of borrow, make it downhill, left to right, and tell yourself it's to win the club championships and there's a fair chance you'll miss. You'll start thinking about outcomes and become tense and nervous. But if you commit yourself to the same physical and mental techniques over and over again you can prevent this from happening.

I start by using progressive physical relaxation. I squeeze the club and tighten my grip from my shoulders, down through my arms and into my fingers. Tighter and tighter I squeeze the club, counting slowly in my mind - one, two, three, four - then I let go and the tension decreases with it, down to a level that I know I can function at.

Don't think I've always concentrated like this; sometimes, in the early part of my career, I had all sorts of problems on the green. I was conscious of forward pressing and I was constantly worried about moving the bottom half of my body as I hit the putt. I struggled to prevent my eyes following the ball, which meant I pulled a lot of putts left. As I've said before, in golf you get what you pay attention to.

Centring does something else for me - it keeps my mood constant, at my optimum level. Sometimes I practise putting with my eyes closed. Try this, it will help you feel balanced and heighten your awareness.

After I've worked out the optimum line and speed, I imagine a bright orange strip along the perfect line, and in my mind I see the ball being dragged into the hole, like water when the bath is emptying. In my mind, I see the ball moving on the line, the speed is perfect, and it drops in at the last moment - the perfect putt, executed exactly right. It doesn't have to be orange; make it whatever colour you want. Experiment. Find out what works for you.

Then, when I come back to the ball, I can still see a brilliant image of an orange line. There are no technical thoughts. My mind is consumed by the target, which my brain thinks I can't miss.

I'm not saying thinking this way is easy. You'll have to work at it. I know for certain that this thought process was a major help in my performance at Japan, playing with the greatest player in the world, in front of thousands of people, holing putts for fun.

Hole More Putts
by Thinking Correctly

Dr. John

When we begin playing golf, we pick up our putting fundamentals without giving the matter much thought. It might be a tip from our pals, something we watched on TV or, better still, a lesson from a professional. Mostly, we are taught to concentrate on our body alignment, the club head, our grip and how to take the putter head away smoothly and on line.

That kind of instruction means that 99 per cent of us become preoccupied with the mechanics of the putting stroke. So we get in our own way and stare obsessively at the head of the putter, our bodies frozen in concentration. Usually, feel will go out of the window and that will have a knock-on effect, which means we'll miss a few putts. When you start missing putts you will think negatively, and, before you know it, you can't hole anything. You will have forgotten what putting is all about - getting the ball into the hole.

Can you imagine a basketball player not concentrating on the ring when he has a free shot? Of course not. And the same applies to just about every other sport. Darters focus on the board, tennis players concentrate on the part of the court they are aiming for and a cricketer, when he is bowling in a Test match, will see a picture in his mind of the stumps. So why should golf be any different?

Another tip that will help you putt better is focusing on the front of the ball. To avoid any confusion, I am talking about the side of the ball that is nearest to the hole. If you focus this way it will help you to impart topspin as the putter head comes through the ball.

You should try using your mind to draw a line on the green on exactly the right route to the hole, taking into account the pace and borrow.

When I worked with Darren Clarke, this was one of the techniques that really paid off for him. He would draw this line in his head as if he was watching the ball move in slow motion replay. Then he just putt the ball down the same line and more often than not, he holed it. Darren's technique was that simple.

I have been helping Englishman Steve Webster recently. Steve produced his best form for three years in the 2004 South African Open at Erinvale when he finished second, behind champion Trevor Immelman. Steve putted superbly all week and in the first round he took just 24 putts on his way to a six-under-par 66.

Before the tournament Steve had been obsessively focusing on his backswing when he putted. I knew he had to stop that way of thinking or he was never going to putt consistently. We achieved this by getting Steve to draw a line along the green from the ball and into the hole. If I remember correctly Steve's line was white, but you can choose any colour you want. So he drew a white line, looked at the front of the ball, the side closest to the hole and hit it. The technique was very simple and that was the main reason he putted great all week.

Line, target and contact. If you can make your putting technique this simple you will definitely improve.

If Tour players could train themselves to look at the hole when they putt they would hole more putts. I admit there can be a downside because there is a risk of not getting the right contact. But if you have good technique you should try putting this way. However, if you aren't comfortable and you have to look at the ball, make sure you focus on the side of the ball that is nearest to the hole. This is vital.

It will help if you can retain an image of the hole inside your head. You should start imagining that every putt is straight. If, for example, you are faced with a big borrow and the line is six inches right of the hole, use your mind to move it. Take a photograph of the hole's new position using an imaginary camera inside your head - keep that picture in your mind, focus on the ball and hit it. If you can do this, your putting will improve dramatically.

Another mental exercise that will help you putt better is a sensible pre-shot routine. We have already discussed the importance of this in your long game. A pre-shot routine is just as important when you putt. Putting is a very precise movement and you must be relaxed when you make your stroke.

Try this. Picture a hole on the correct line, aim yourself accordingly, focus on the front of the ball (the side closest to the hole) and imagine making a clean stroke. Remember it is important to focus on the front, not the back. That will help you put topspin on the ball and keep it on line. Never focus on the putter head or you will always be inconsistent

Dean Robertson is one of the best putters on the European Tour. He's been regularly ranked in the top ten Tour statistics for putting for almost 10 years. Dean uses a technique called centring. He focuses on his stomach and then the front of the ball, which gets him relaxed and stable. That's the key to his terrific putting on Tour. He has a sixth sense that the ball can't miss and that produces confidence which, in turn, produces relaxation and before your know it you're holing everything.

Think of the greatest putt you have ever made. Use your mind to relive the moment, make it real and that will allow you to enjoy wonderful, positive sensations such as joy and fulfilment. When that feeling overwhelms you, make the putt. All of us have experienced a feeling when we knew instinctively that we were going to make a certain putt. It's an inexplicable premonition that just falls on us out of the sky when we least expect it. If you use the power of your mind to think correctly, you can recall that uplifting sensation more often.

You can use history to help you too. Most golfers will remember that great 15-foot putt that Irishman Paul McGinley holed at The Belfry in 2002 to win the Ryder Cup for the Europeans. I can still see Paul jumping in the air and being swamped by the rest of the team. You can imagine you're him. Picture yourself inside Paul's body, see the crowd and imagine how he felt when the ball disappeared into the hole and he had secured his place in golfing history for all time. You will draw on all the wonderful sensations he was feeling. That will relax you and help you hole more putts.

Think of your brain as a computer. Make all the calculations necessary to hole the putt and programme your computer brain accordingly. This will include bombarding your mind with all the positive thoughts that will relax and help you. If your thinking revolves around feeling nervous, missing putts, thinking about outcomes and pressure, you don't need me to tell you that the inevitable conclusion will be a missed putt. That's guaranteed.

Putting is no different to any other part of the game. You will putt better if you access positive feelings from your memory of occasions when you were holing everything. The memories will all be there, inside your mind. It's just a case of accessing them and using these positive feelings whenever you want

So before you putt, think of a really great putt you have made - it might be earlier in the round, a week before or even 10 years ago. It doesn't matter. What does matter is thinking how you felt when the ball dropped into the hole. I'll bet you can't hold back a smile because you will be feeling so good.

Then use your mind to draw an imaginary line to the hole in whatever colour you like, focus on the front of the ball and putt. That would be a perfect routine for everyone, from a 24-handicapper to a Tour player.

Use the power of your mind and you can putt like a champion.

Summary
Putting doesn't have to be complicated. Try to think of it like this - line, target, contact. Yes, it is that simple. Get an image of the hole into your brain, use your mind to draw a line on the green, focus on the front of the ball and putt. Alternatively, if you have good technique, try looking at the hole when you actually make your stroke.

Allow your eyes to make all the calculations and I'm convinced you'll putt better. Putting should be a simple process yet lots of Tour players focus on the wrong things, such as the club head or shoulders or hands. Remember more than a third of your shots are taken on the green. Think wisely and improve your putting and your handicap will come tumbling down.

CHAPTER TEN

How your Imagination
Can Help you

Dean

I have played many times with three of the world's greatest flair players – Severiano Ballesteros, Jose-Maria Olazabal and Sergio Garcia. It's no co-incidence that they are Spaniards. Most Latin people are expressive like that – Italian Constantino Rocca is another who comes to mind. They even use their hands to express themselves when they talk to you. As for on the golf course, well, they're something special, aren't they?

When I was growing up in the early 80s, I remember watching Seve playing Arnold Palmer at Wentworth in the World Matchplay Championships. Seve was in all sorts of trouble on the 18th but he holed an 80-yard shot from under some rhododendron bushes for an eagle three to save his match. It didn't cross anyone's mind that he would even contemplate such a shot. Everyone thought Seve would chip out sideways and try to make his par with a pitch and a putt. That's what the percentage play would have been. It was a ridiculous shot really, but that was Seve all over - he did that sort of thing all the time.

You may recall a couple of years earlier, when Seve fulfilled his lifetime's ambition by winning the Open Championship at Royal Lytham & St Annes. He was smashing his driver all over the place. He was so wild, his nickname for a while after the tournament was 'the car park champion'. It didn't matter where he hit his tee shots; somehow he always found a way to recover. It was a similar story when he won the Open again, five years later at St Andrew's.

Seve was a couple of shots behind Tom Watson playing the 17th, a hole ahead of the American in the final round. Seve hooked his tee shot on the Road Hole into the left-hand rough, leaving an impossible shot for any normal player. But Seve isn't normal. He is a genius.

Seve took out his seven iron and lashed the ball, hooking it an incredible amount, sidespin driving the ball forward, 70 yards short of the green before rolling on and on and finishing 20 feet from the pin. In the circumstances the shot was nothing short of miraculous. So Seve got his par on the toughest hole on the course. It was a different story for Tom, following Seve. Tom hit a perfect drive on the right of the fairway but then took too much club and leaked his second to the right of the green, where the ball rolled onto the road and an inevitable bogey followed.

The rest, as they say, is history. Seve went on to birdie the final hole and take the championship but it was his incredible seven iron to the 17th green that broke Tom's heart and earned the Spaniard the title.

Who can forget Sergio Garcia bursting on the scene as a young teenager and battling Tiger Woods in the 1999 US PGA Championships at Medina? Sergio put the heat on Tiger with a miraculous shot from the roots of a tree. He had to cut the ball around the trunk; in fact, the shot was so tough I thought Sergio might have broken his wrists. I'm sure you can remember him running up the fairway after the ball, jumping up in the air with excitement, a great big smile of accomplishment on his face.

Jose-Maria Olazabal has won the US Masters twice and both times he was all over the place from the tee, and in the trees constantly. But somehow, most of the time, Jose-Maria conjured up a spectacular shot the rest of us couldn't have contemplated. He made blind shots, shots round, through and over trees and lakes. Looking back it was almost a nonsense he won those titles, but that's genius for you. These players will always find a way. If Jose-Maria could hit more fairways now, he could still win more Majors.

Seve, Sergio and Jose-Maria are all notoriously bad drivers. But if you put a huge, wide oak tree in the middle of a fairway, they would find a way to get the ball round, under or over – somehow they would hit the fairway. It might take a banana hook or a big slice – it wouldn't matter. Their imagination would find a way.

Yet if you ask them to hit a ball down a narrow fairway into a small space, they would often find trouble, a lot more regularly than less able players who don't have their genius. It's all down to their visualisation and imagination, seeing the shots the rest of us wouldn't have the ability to try.

They're crowd-pleasers. Everyone likes to watch them because they are so unpredictable. They thrive on the challenges. Other Tour players are down the middle and hitting greens, holing the odd putt and shooting good scores, but these three, well, no-one knows what they are going to do next. Australian Greg Norman has been like that too. Sandy Lyle was another. Fans love them.

Before I met Dr. John Pates I could be a creative player in certain circumstances. But it was instinctive. I couldn't explain to you how it worked.

In 1989 I was in the final of the Scottish Foursomes Championship at Paisley Golf Club, partnering my good friend Brian Park. On the sixth hole in the final Brian hit a bad hook into the trees. The poor guy was disgusted with himself. He felt he'd let me down. Don't forget this was foursomes – alternative shots with one ball.

Brian just expected me to chip the ball out sideways and hope for a chip and a putt. I could see another way though: I was down by the ball, weighing everything up, and I could see this tiny gap under the branches of one tree and over another. I would say the gap, which was about 10 yards away, was a maximum of two square feet, the size of a small window in your bathroom.

I called Brian over and at first he dismissed my plans and told me to chip the ball out onto the fairway. "Look at that wee gap," I told him. "I can do it."

He didn't look convinced but he nodded his head. I took out my seven iron, made a few practise swings and we decided to have a go. After all it was matchplay and whatever happened we could only lose one hole.

I hit the shot perfectly, the ball sneaking on the green where we went on to par the hole for a half. We eventually won the title and that creative shot out of the trees was one of the defining moments of the final.

So even at 19 I knew I had creative instincts but I didn't know how my mind worked and all the mental tools I could call on when I needed to try something out of the ordinary.

Moving on 11 years, to 2003 and now I'm an experienced professional on the European Tour playing in the

Malaysian Open at the Mines Resort and Golf Club, Kuala Lumpur. The pressures are massively increased but now, thanks to Dr. John, I know how to think to help me pull off one of the hardest shots I have ever faced, just when I need it most.

It was the 72nd hole and I was high up on the leaderboard. I leaked my tee shot to the right, and, out of the rough, I hit a huge flyer over the green, between two grandstands.

You can imagine the situation now - thousands of people were watching, the TV cameras were there and there was a huge amount of cash at stake. Standing on my toes I could just see the top of the flag, the lie was terrible and there was a massive slope on the green. I was staring a double bogey in the face.

I chose a landing area on the fringe of the green, no bigger than a handkerchief - I had to be that accurate. Because I couldn't see the green it was tough to visualise the shot so I imagined I was floating above myself, perhaps 20 feet in the air looking down. It was so much easier from up there because now I'm seeing everything I need on my own mental television screen - the ball, the pin, myself and my caddy Brian.

I visualised myself playing the shot just right. I watched myself standing over the ball, the club moving away rhythmically, the ball landing in the perfect place, taking the borrow and rolling around the contours before it stopped a few inches from the hole. Looking at myself and the shot from above, gave me a feel for exactly what the ball would do and where I needed to pitch it on the fringe of the green.

I'm over the ball now, going over my mental and physical discipline you've already heard about - pre-shot routine, external imagery and focus. Now I add the picture of the perfect shot just a moment before I play. This also helps calm my nerves. Thinking this way made it easy to disassociate myself from the pressure and the importance of the shot. I executed the shot perfectly, pitching the ball on exactly the right place and I just had time to run up the bank and watch the ball circling down towards the pin, on and on, taking the borrow until it popped out of sight into the hole for a birdie. What a bonus. I had been dead and buried and now I'd played this miraculous shot under all that pressure.

That birdie allowed me to finish on 18-under, a couple of shots behind champion Arjun Atwal. I'd shot 66 in the final round to finish fourth and pick up a cheque for £36,000. If I had fluffed the shot and made a bogey I would have dropped down the field and lost £10,000.

You may not be fortunate enough to play on the Tour but everything is relative. We all have our own goals and targets. The pressure for you will be same, whether it is to break 80 for the first time, win the club championship or par the 18th to cut your handicap.

So you might not be able to play the same as a Tour player but with a bit of work you can think like him. Then you'll find it much easier to fulfil your dreams.

How your Imagination Can Help

Dr. John

If you close your eyes and think of an image, perhaps a pleasant memory of an enjoyable holiday or a programme you saw recently on television, you are accessing the right side of your brain. You will not be aware of it, but using your brain's 'right side' is the only way you can get 'into the zone', and play your best golf.

Your left brain is all about evaluation and problem solving, and your right brain is used for imagination and creation. Your left brain is scientific and analytical and your right brain is artistic and instinctive.

The right side of your brain also controls your speed, rhythm and tempo when you are performing a task. So if you access your right side, you are guaranteed to swing a golf club more freely and as a result be more successful. Your swing will be smoother and we all know how important that rhythm is to good golf.

If you want to improve your game it is paramount that you use your imagination. That will automatically allow you to access your creative side. Imagery will also help you control your emotions. You need to start thinking about positive experiences you have enjoyed rather than negative ones, which can destroy you. We all struggle to stop thinking this way - missed putts and wild drives are hard to forget, especially when we are playing in an important tournament. I'm going to teach you how you can control the way you think.

Englishman Chris Gane is a fine young golfer but like a lot of players on Tour, he has never quite fulfilled his potential. I was working with Chris a couple of years ago in the Smurfit European Open which was being played at Ireland's K Club.

Well, right out of the blue, he began playing the best golf of his life. I always knew he had bags of talent but I wasn't prepared for the way he started the tournament. Chris was six-under-par after 10 holes of the opening round - he was actually leading the championship, and this was obviously unfamiliar territory to him. There he was, on top of the leaderboard - Chris Gane, six-under - ahead of some of the world's greatest players.

The television cameras appeared from nowhere as TV journalists sensed a big story breaking - there was a buzz in the crowd each time he holed a putt. Chris had been effortlessly playing 'in his zone' but suddenly, all this commotion snapped him out of it. He stopped playing using his artistic right brain and began playing with his analytical left brain.

Chris told me what had happened afterwards. He said he had an idea in his head that his swing wouldn't look good on television. Chris tried hard but he couldn't shake off the feelings. He began to think his swing might be embarrassing to him. So his whole mind-set changed completely. He stopped thinking freely, without pressure or technical thoughts. And as a result he really struggled on the back nine, not because he was swinging badly but because he was thinking badly. Chris had two bogeys and a double bogey on his way to a 69, which still put him well up on the leaderboard. Sadly he couldn't regain that sensational form he had displayed on the front nine and he finished well off the pace. New Zealander Michael Campbell took the title on six-under-par which shows how tough the course was.

Chris had got into an evaluating and judgmental way of thinking. He forgot to think creatively by using imagery.

If you are in a positive frame of mind, you should use what we call 'internal imagery.' That will allow you to amplify those feelings. You start focusing on the images you see in your mind's eye. But if you use internal imagery when you are not feeling confident you could be in trouble. If you are feeling negative - for example suffering from nerves, bad temper, frustration or pressure, your destructive feelings will be amplified and you are certain to play poorly. That's guaranteed.

It's a strange thing, but if a Tour player is feeling angry or under pressure he can still hit his driver well. Hitting the ball a long way requires a state of mind that involves aggressive and powerful emotions. But the nearer the green he gets, the tougher it will be. If the player doesn't use his imagination to control those aggressive feelings his short game will be all over the place. Pitching, chipping and putting require fine control movements and obviously needs a different way of thinking to blasting a drive a long way down a wide fairway.

So if you are experiencing emotions such as anger, nerves and frustration, your feel and touch will suffer badly. And they will have a particularly bad effect on your putting. This is when you should use 'external imagery'.

You should imagine you are outside your body, as if you are having a dream. See yourself from another person's point of view, perhaps as if you are in a crowd watching yourself play. You can practise this at home. Thinking this way will enable you to reduce those negative feelings that are hurting you. You might even get rid of them altogether. That's because you will be in a 'disassociative state'. You will be distancing yourself from the situation and the further away you can get, the more powerful the process will be and all those bad feelings should disappear.

External imagery is a great technique for getting rid of your negative thoughts. This is an awesome way of controlling your golf swing too. Our primary source of learning as children is imitation. We learn everything by imitating the people around us - our fathers, mothers, brothers and sisters and the rest of our family and friends. That's how we learnt to walk, to speak, to kick a football and tie our shoelaces.

Let's look at an example. If you are hitting balls on a golf range and you are struggling with tempo and timing, try creating an external image of yourself. Imagine you are outside your body looking at yourself. If this concept is difficult for you to understand, it might help if you imagine there is a television inside your head and you are looking at yourself on the screen. In this image you could be seeing yourself from a variety of different angles. You might be directly behind yourself, looking up the fairway or you could be watching yourself from the side. Experiment; whatever you feel most comfortable with will work the best. Play the swing you want to see on the television screen inside your head. Make it the most perfect swing you have made in your life, and see the ball soaring into the distance, landing by the flag - then hit your shot. Use the image as a trigger.

This is a fantastic method to use if you are nervous. You will hit the ball better. Another 'trick' that works for a lot of my Tour players is using their imagination to see the image in slow motion. When you do that your swing will slow down too and your tempo will improve. You can incorporate this whole mental process into your pre-shot routine.

Try this. I'm sure you will have been in a horrible pot bunker at some point in your golfing career and wondered how you were going to get the ball out. Some of these bunkers are so deep you can't even see the flag. The 17th Road Hole at St Andrews has a greenside bunker like that. Every time an Open Championship is held on the Old Course some of the world's greatest players make a hash of it. If I remember correctly, American David Duval took four or five shots to get his ball out of that awful bunker a couple of years ago.

So getting out of a pot bunker is a tough shot for anyone, even a top Tour player. You can't picture where to pitch the ball, can you? This should help. Try seeing yourself in this internal TV set we have been talking about, standing alongside the flag, holding it. Then imagine the ball coming out of the bunker, rolling down the green and into the hole. Keep the image in your mind then hit the ball. Nine times out of 10 you'll play a better shot. This is a great example of how you can use your imagination to improve your golf.

External imagery will bring enjoyment back to your golf. The next time you play, try to think of the target before you hit the ball and then focus on an external image of your swing. Line yourself up to the target and picture it in your mind. If you are one of those players who feels comfortable thinking about technique, create a picture of your perfect swing then hit the ball. If you have been swinging too quickly, make your image move in slow motion. And if you have been struggling with the strike, then focus on the clubhead actually hitting the ball - make it perfect, then hit the shot.

That's how Masters champion Ian Woosnam thinks all the time - strike, pitch mark - strike, pitch mark - that's all he concentrates on when he's playing. You can learn from Woosie by focusing on a particular element of the image. Don't see the whole swing; just concentrate on the part of the movement you are struggling with. Think of your mind as a computer programme that can't go wrong if you think the right way. And that means right brain thinking.

Imagery is the cornerstone of good golf. Jack Nicklaus talked about imagery in his book *Golf My Way*, which was written 30 years ago. He said imagery was the most important mental skill in his bag. Jack would never hit any shot without seeing a picture of the shot in his mind first. He could visualise the shape of his shots, perhaps a fade or a draw - and that's external imagery.

Fred Couples is the same. His favourite mental technique is to think of a great shot he has hit previously. He might see himself hitting a monstrous drive or holing an eight-iron or chipping in - whatever the shot was he was faced with, he'd call on his vast memory to come up with an appropriate shot. That's one of the main reasons Fred has been such a great champion. Thinking that way reinforces all the positive images he already has.

Watching top players succeed will help you too. That's called modelling. Watch Els and Woods on the TV and imagine what it's like to play like them. See yourself inside their body swinging the club perfectly. If you can do that your golf will improve beyond your wildest dreams.

Summary

You should use internal imagery when you are feeling good about your game and external imagery when you are feeling negative. External imagery will help you to feel neutral - you won't feel particularly good and you won't feel particularly bad. That means you will play as if you are on the driving range and nothing is at stake and we already know how beneficial such relaxed thinking can be to you.

You will have to experiment to find out which kind of image will help you. Many players like to see a picture in their mind from behind the ball looking towards the target but others like to see themselves from the side so the target is not visible and all they are seeing is this perfect swing. Use your imagination to get what you want and your golf will improve dramatically.

CHAPTER ELEVEN

How Stephen Gallacher Shot Nine-Under-Par for 14 Holes

Stephen Gallacher

Professional golfers who are playing badly do not make good company. They are to be avoided. Conversation with struggling players may start innocently on a general topic of conversation such as soccer or the fuel economy of the Ford Mondeo, but the subject matter quickly returns to missed cuts and blocked drives.

Other Tour players, unless they are close friends, make a point of keeping out of their way, as if mediocre performances are infectious, a rare and unpleasant virus that could be picked up in the same way you catch a cold.

Players in a slump find it difficult to manufacture confidence. They believe that feeling good about their game is a long process that can take days or weeks or even months. The professional golfer who is susceptible to negative self-analysis, sees confidence through the eyes of a competent builder erecting a house without assistance.

And every time he conducts a satisfactory session on the range or successfully holes a difficult putt, in his mind they are individual bricks layed skilfully, small but important steps on the way to completing his house of confidence.

After a while he'll risk telling anyone who'll listen that he's 'hitting the ball well' or that 'I'm really popping my new driver'. And for a short time, usually no longer than a few days, he'll find he's 'in the zone' and shooting low. Then it all goes wrong. His house of confidence is blown away by a theoretical hurricane and he's left sifting through the rubble searching for an answer, and a quick way to 'get back in the zone', his confidence evaporated in an instant like sticking a pin in a balloon. Pop! And he's back at the range blasting balls and looking despairingly for a technical solution.

Scottish international Stephen Gallacher was in a slump when he arrived at the Italian Open at Olgiata Golf Club, just outside Rome. He had survived just two cuts from his previous 11 tournaments and finished 103rd, 101st and joint 106th in three of his last four events. Golf journalists found it impossible to prevent themselves from referring to his form as 'disappointing' and he was developing a nagging reputation for unfulfilled potential.

Stephen turned professional in 1994 when his handicap was plus four, which means he was so good he had to add four shots to his final total. He enjoyed an amateur career you would die for. Stephen played off scratch when he was 16 and won dozens of tournaments including the Scottish Boys Championships (twice), the Scottish Amateur, the Scottish Youths, the European Championship and the Lytham Trophy. But now, after nine years with the big boys, he had not won a tournament and self-doubt had begun to erode his ability.

"When I was an amateur, I was winning everything," says Stephen. "Whenever I turned up, I expected to win.

In fact, I knew I was going to win, even when I wasn't playing well. I had to get back into that frame of mind as a pro but I didn't know where to start. Then I met sports psychologist Dr. John Pates and my whole life changed.

"I'd seen this big guy around the Tour and, to be honest, I thought he was a rep for Titleist. My pal Gary Emerson had introduced us the week before the Italian Open in Rome. I told Dr. John I was struggling and that I needed to sort out my mind but I hadn't seen the right person.

"I hadn't played well for two months. I was trying too hard and getting in my own way, forcing everything and getting nervous. We chatted for 15 minutes on the putting green and I liked what he was saying. It was all so simple and made such good sense."

Dr. John and Stephen had talked briefly several times over the previous few days, often just for a few minutes. The total amount of time they had spent together did not exceed one hour but it had provided information that enabled Dr. John to identify the areas Stephen had to work on to improve his form.

Firstly, and most importantly, he had developed an irrational faith in technique so that he was unable to hit a ball without the comfort of concentrating on positions and swing thoughts, which just happened to be the opposite of what he should be doing - freeing his mind.

No matter how hard Stephen tried to eradicate negative thoughts when he was not playing well, they would return without warning, nibbling away at the edges of his mind, reminding him of that three-foot putt he missed the week before or the blocked drive that careered out of bounds.

Stephen had also found it difficult to 'get in the zone' - a positive state of mind he found so effortlessly as a young amateur. Finally, his pre-shot routine had become unpredictable and erratic.

"I admit I was very technically minded," says Stephen. "As an amateur, I just went for all my shots. I'd hole more putts because I wasn't worried about my stroke - I just picked the line and whacked it. But when I turned pro I started to think about the line and read too much into it. I was steering the ball and I had become scared in case I missed.

"Bob Torrance was my coach back then and he was really good at motivating. He would say to me, 'You're the best and you're ready' - you know, stuff like that.

"A guy called Dr. John Mathers came to help the Scottish squad about 10 years ago but a lot of the players laughed at him because none of us had done anything like that before.

"As for when I played in the Walker Cup, well, there was no psychology at all. We all thought it was a backward step. We just played - that was it. For me it was all about swinging well and hitting the ball. If I was hitting my driver well, then I would play well. It went right through my game.

"I knew I had to get that feeling back but I didn't know how."

The two men had much to talk about. Back in Madrid, they had made an agreement to work together, at some unspecified time in the future. This meeting on the putting green in Italy had been unplanned, but Stephen was determined to make the most of it.

"I'm going to hit a few balls on the range before I tee off. Will you come with me, Dr. John?" he asked.

Stephen loosened up and began hitting nine irons with purpose, timing his shots adequately but not perfectly and certainly not to the preposterously high standards of a European Tour player who has won more than £600,000.

"What are you thinking about before you play a shot?" asked Dr. John.

"Well, actually, I'm trying to make sure my club is just a touch outside the line on the backswing," Stephen said, with a sense of accomplishment.

"Oh, yes," said Dr. John, sternly.

Stephen continued: "That's something I'm working on with my coach at the moment."

"Tell me," said Dr. John. "When was the last really good shot you hit under pressure? When were you last in the zone?"

It was an easy answer. The week before, in Madrid, Stephen had just six holes of the second round to play and he was one shot inside the cut. All he had to do was par in and he knew he would be playing at the weekend, a considerable accomplishment considering his recent form. Then he had a six, two-over-par, the result of a clumsy mistake, so he needed to birdie two of the last four holes or he would be packing his suitcase early - an unpleasant task he had become familiar with.

"I needed to make the cut in Spain to keep my card," Stephen said. "After that double bogey, I had to make two birdies, which made me angry and got me up a bit. On the next hole I hit it to four feet for an eagle and although I missed the putt, I wasn't worried.

"Then I just missed the green on the 17th. I looked at the shot and somehow I just knew I was going to hole it. I looked at my caddy and said: 'This is going in.' I took out my lob wedge and that was it - in it went. I've always been able to do that when I really needed to."

Dr. John smiled and said: "Don't you think it would be better to play in that frame of mind all the time instead of thinking about technique? You can. Just concentrate. Get an image in your mind of holing that chip and how you felt. Recall all those good feelings."

So Stephen closed his eyes and returned to the 17th green at Madrid. He recalled the striped shirt his caddie was wearing and the statistical information of the hole in question, which was a 374-yard par four, dogleg to the right.

He saw his wedge approach shot, which he pushed slightly, just a hint but enough for the ball to drift to the right, missing the green by no more than a yard, perhaps 20 feet from the hole.

Stephen is alongside his caddy now, with a lob wedge in his hand, crouching down, concentrating, seeing the line perfectly and the ball's moving along the green on its predetermined path towards the hole, as if it is being sucked in by an invisible force. In it went, his caddy thumps his fist in the air, the memory real, the sensation so powerful a smile of satisfaction works its way across his face.

He felt good. Confident. Invincible.

"Now hit a shot," said Dr. John.

So he did. And the ball soared in the air, straight as an arrow, landing softly alongside the pin fluttering softly in the distance 130 yards away, backspin zipping it back gently a few feet. Stephen went through the same routine again and again, each time moving in his mind back to Madrid and returning to the present in an instant, positive thoughts flooding through his brain.

He changed clubs several times but the result was always the same, an effortless swing he did not think about, the ball flying obediently to the target. He had an image of being inside a mechanical robot on a car assembly line, completing a complicated task efficiently, over and over again.

A tentative smile of appreciation spread across his face and Stephen announced boldly: "Right, I'm going to use this today, on the course. I'm ready." The two men shook hands warmly, the teacher and pupil, celebrating a job well done.

Stephen headed towards the first tee, where a large crowd awaited him, non-golfers mainly, dark-skinned Italians puffing cigarettes, drinking cans of Coca-Cola and looking cool in their designer sun glasses.

He had a spring in his step, an excitement he had not felt for some time. Stephen now believed he could get in the zone whenever it was necessary and that confidence was a natural force of energy he could tap into at will, like plugging in an electric kettle.

Brian Davies and Robert Karlsson, his partners for the first round, were waiting for him. Stephen was not familiar with such positive thoughts. The first tee can be a daunting place for a professional golfer without confidence. He is aware of the crowd, the pressure and the indignities a difficult course can subject him to. But not today.

The first hole at Olgiata is a tight par-four of 378 yards with a narrow fairway the width of a country road and a green smaller than Peggy Mitchell's living room, surrounded by bunkers. Stephen's name was announced to the crowd, who stopped talking instantly, the silence eerie and unsettling.

He pulled out his driver, took a short mental trip back to his chip-in at Madrid, focused on the ball, then the target and away it went, his cocoon of concentration broken by the applause of the crowd, clapping enthusiastically, a hint of awe in their actions as the ball exploded into the distance, splitting the fairway more than 300 yards away.

That drive was the first step in the reconstruction of his career. He went on to shoot 69, three under par, and two ahead of Ryder Cup hero Padraig Harrington. Stephen repeated the round on the second day and made the cut comfortably despite the constant threat of a thunderstorm which eventually exploded onto the course and forced tournament officials to reduce the event to 54 holes.

Now he could concentrate on making money, which would be certain to test his new mental skills as he came down the stretch, aware as he always was that a single missed putt could cost him more cash than a nurse earns in a year.

Stephen was ready.

He discussed his opening two rounds with his caddy, Irishman Dermot Byrne, over a beer in the clubhouse. They concluded that his game was good, excellent in fact, and that he was capable of 'shooting the lights out' and recording a really low total.

Stephen started the final round disappointingly with two bogeys in the first four holes - then it happened. He birdied five of the next six holes to go out in 34. He went on to birdie the 10th, eagle the 15th and birdie the 16th and 17th before parring the 18th to finish with 65, seven-under-par or rather nine-under-par for 14 holes. He had taken 25 putts and his average drive had improved from

293 yards in the first round to 313 yards in the final round.

"I was two-over after four but I was determined to stick with my new routine," Stephen says. "I hadn't shot nine-under for 14 holes for years not since I was an amateur. It came right out of the blue. I wasn't thinking about my score, just the target, my routine, my zone and hitting the ball."

Stephen's finishing total was 13-under-par and just six shots behind the champion Ian Poulter, who blew everyone away in the first round with an incredible 61. Stephen picked up £13,000, his highest cheque for 19 tournaments. He finished 10th, his highest finish for almost a year, but more importantly his success had proved to him that the old Stephen had gone forever. And he wasn't coming back.

⌒

"It's so simple yet I'd never done it before," says Stephen, looking back. "It was like a light being switched on. On the range we started concentrating on targets and good shots that I'd hit sometime in the past, shots that were important at the time. I felt brilliant when I chipped in in Madrid, so I thought about that and the difference was amazing. In fact I just couldn't hit a bad shot on the range.

"Before that, on the first tee all my thoughts were about technique and if I played badly I'd try something else, then something else - but nothing worked. A lot of Tour players think like that.

"If I had hit the ball badly on the range, I would be worried on the first tee. Now it doesn't matter to me. I just go on the tee and hit it - I don't worry any more.

"Confidence can go in two shots if you're thinking of technique. I had got into the habit of thinking negatively - 'let's just get it off the tee, let's hit it away from the trouble' - that's the sort of thing I'd say to myself. Now I just think of the shot in front of me and where I want the ball to go. Your parameters come right in and if you hit a bad shot it will be 10 yards off line, not 50."

Stephen's improvement continued towards the end of the year and into the early part of the following season, most notably in the Heineken Classic at Royal Melbourne.

He finished fourth, with a four-round total of 12-under-par, and earned £28,000, one of the highest pay cheques of his nine-year career. He had many reasons to celebrate, especially his magnificent final round of 65, seven-under-par and the lowest round of the day.

"I've always felt that I'm a better player than my results suggest and that I have a lot of potential," he says. "I knew all about the zone, but that only happened to me every now and then.

"But now, thanks to Dr. John, I'm in the zone every time I play. Dr. John has taught me how to think like that all the time, even if I'm not hitting the ball well. Now, when I get over the ball I just think of my target. My goal is to get into contention every week.

"Tiger Woods is the best in the world mentally. He's been doing that since he was 12 years old. Every Tour player can hit good shots but with Tiger, well, under pressure, every time he goes out he expects to win.

"His routine is perfect, his swing is perfect and he's athletic. But he's also the best mentally and that's no coincidence. It makes him the best in the world.

What really separates him from the rest are his mental strength and his routine. He doesn't think about things over the ball.

"If I had played with Tiger before I met Dr. John, I would probably have tried too hard and I'd end up forcing shots. I'd probably be working on my swing out there on the course, too. Now I think I could cope. I would just go through my routine. Yes, I would be nervous. Who wouldn't? Even Woods gets nervous, but it's all about channelling your feelings the right way."

The change in the way Stephen views his career and future prospects has been spectacular. And there is powerful and conclusive numerical evidence published by the European Tour press office which makes pleasant reading as he ponders the new season.

Stephen's stroke average had improved from the previous year from 72.61 (143rd) to 70.86 (80th), which is the best part of a seven-shot reduction per tournament, which is the difference between a Ferrari and a Ford Focus and means he could seriously contemplate contending and ultimately winning tournaments.

There are other encouraging changes throughout his game, including a seven-yard increase in driving distance. But the most revealing statistic is Stephen's incredible improvement in driving accuracy, such a vital component of low scores.

Professional golfers who miss fairways do not make sufficient money. They miss more greens, find more bunkers, take more putts and end up contemplating a dramatic career change selling motor cars or peddling double glazing.

With the help of Dr. John Pates, Stephen has increased his driving accuracy from 62.2 per cent (71st) to 78.1 per cent (fifth), which means he is hitting two more fairways every round, enabling him to record fewer bogeys and more birdies.

"I was stuck in a rut and I obviously wanted to get in contention and win a tournament. But I was getting in my own way. Now my technique has improved thanks to my coach Adam Hunter. I'm focused now but I wasn't then and I knew it was all down to the mental game. The trouble was I didn't know who to see.

"I remember asking all the top guys on the Tour how important they thought the mental game was to them and they all said it was a really big factor. Open champion Paul Lawrie has worked on his mind for the last five years and he told me it was pivotal to his success. I started thinking to myself that I had never done that so there must be something wrong.

"I've always had people telling me that I should be winning and there's nothing worse because that puts pressure on you. I don't want to be one of those guys who could have done better. I know now I might hit the ball in the rough or in the trees. Everyone does. What is important is how I react to it.

"I've got just five GCEs and before I met Dr. John I found all this stuff double Dutch. I tried reading psychology books but it all went over my head. Now things are looking good and I can't wait for the season to start."

When Stephen looks back at how he used to be, chasing the perfect swing, focusing on out-of-bounds fences and pot bunkers, he smiles to himself, looking ahead to all the low scores he's going shoot and all the money he's going to accumulate, as if he can't quite believe life could ever be quite this good.

How Stephen Gallacher Shot Nine-Under-Par for 14 Holes

Dr. John

Tour players like Stephen Gallacher come to sports psychologists for one thing – to get into the zone. The trouble is they don't know how to get there. Every now and then they'll shoot a low score but they lack consistency. So they come to me to find out what the zone is, how it works and how to tap into it, so they can transform normal levels of accomplishment.

Professional golfers know if they get in the zone they are more likely to play well, perhaps even win a European Tour tournament, but their needs are exactly the same as the requirements of high handicappers - it's just that their goals and expectations are different. Stephen Gallacher wants to win a European Tour event and earn the £150,000 cheque that might go with it, whereas a club golfer wants to cut his handicap or win the monthly medal. Either way they won't fulfil their potential without getting in the zone more often.

So what is the zone? Well, there are lots of factors and every golfer will have experienced them many times but usually by accident. You'll find yourself in the zone, without warning, usually after hitting a good shot. It will enable you to play well, probably superbly. It might last one shot or one hole, and if you're lucky it could continue for a week but one thing is certain. You'll fall out of your zone and you won't know how to get back in.

When a player is in the zone he does not think about technical thoughts, and most importantly he'll be having fun. The player will experience high levels of energy and feelings of power and he will be in complete control. He is calm, mentally and physically, and he'll be over-whelmed by a feeling of confidence. Players are not all the same though. Some experience what I call 'calm aggression,' so they are on a high when they are in the zone and they need high levels of stimulation to play their best. That kind of player is not common, though. Most of us play better when we reduce the pressure and experience calm.

A Tour player can usually get into the zone after he has hit a particularly good shot. They are all looking for one great shot which will allow them to experience positive feelings which often enables the player to put together a string of birdies. You see this time and time again on the leaderboards on the Tour around the world. And there's a reason for it.

Good shots are associated with certain emotions. But players get things the wrong way round. If they learnt how to access the emotions first they'd hit more good shots and shoot lower scores.

When I first met Stephen Gallacher he told me he hadn't been playing well for some time. The week before, in Madrid, he had just scraped enough money to keep his Tour card for the following season. There had been a recent bereavement in the family so he wasn't feeling too good, which was, of course, understandable.

We started talking about what went on in his mind when he played his best. We worked out a pre-shot routine which allowed him to experience the kind of emotions he felt when he was in his zone. We called it 'his bubble.'

Firstly we had to remove all technical thoughts when he is on the course, especially in a tournament and even more especially when he is actually swinging the club. Stephen was a great pupil who had faith in our plan.

Stephen's old pre-shot routine involved a set of movements that was designed to aim him correctly at the target - you've all read the books, everything square to the line - clubhead, feet, hips and shoulders. That's great but he wasn't aiming his mind.

If you asked a taxi driver to take you to a house in Birmingham, he might get within 20 or 30 miles of your destination but you would never arrive without telling him the area, street and number. Well, your mind is the same. You have to get your mind to line up with the target as well as your body and clubface.

Stephen started to focus really hard on his target, whether it was the pin or a particular spot on the fairway he wanted the ball to finish. He took a snapshot of the image as if he had a mental camera inside his head that froze the scene so he could access a still, colour photograph clearly in his mind. So when he looked away from the target and back at the ball he would see the target clearly in his mind.

That mental picture forced out all the other thoughts that had prevented him from playing his best. This made it impossible for Stephen to think about outcomes, bad shots or technical thoughts, all the things that had paralysed him before and made him miss nine cuts from 11 tournaments.

All those feelings can destroy you. Evaluation and concentrating on technique instead of mental pictures is what is known as 'left brain activity.' The left side of your brain controls language, evaluation and problem solving. Of course, golfers don't know this, but they need to recognise that it is impossible to get in the zone unless you stop thinking this way.

The right side of the brain is all about art, creativity and is based on imagery. This is what you should be using to play golf and is the reason geniuses like Seve Ballesteros and Lee Trevino have been so successful. They are artists.

So how can we achieve that? It would be great if we had a switch on the side of our heads so we could turn from one to another, like clicking from AM to FM on your radio. Obviously we can't do that but if you understand how your brain works, you can learn how to control it, and then you can get in the zone and fulfil your goals.

You use your left brain when you write out a shopping list and when you tick off the tins of beans and biscuits as you place them in your basket. The right brain is all about art, so you use this if you draw or paint or kick a football, anything that is creative.

If you are in a music shop contemplating a CD and you choose Robbie Williams instead of Elton Dr. John, that's the left brain. But when you get home and play the album and experience pleasure, that's your right brain.

The right brain controls the rhythm, speed and tempo of motor movements, which happens to be precisely what you are trying to do when you are attempting to hit a golf ball.

So if you can shift activity to the right brain you are much more likely to make a better swing, a better contact and a better shot. But that's not all.

You will 'quieten' the part of your mind that could make you worry about out of bounds or lakes or the cash you might lose to your partners if you don't hole that five-foot putt. The left brain creates anxiety.

We define our emotions and our world through language. So if you shut down language it is impossible to worry. You can't think to yourself ' my swing is terrible' or 'these clubs are not good for me.' Shut down your left brain and you will throw away all the stuff that creates problems in every sport.

Tour players are the same as club golfers. When they play badly it is almost always because they think badly, when they concentrate on technique or when they start to worry about outcomes, such as if they are going to make the cut, how much money it might cost them or perhaps a bad shot they might have hit earlier in the round in similar circumstances.

Thinking of bad shots will kill you. That will make you think negatively, and then you'll hit another bad shot, then another and another. Your game is finished.

So how does the handicap player use this information to improve his game? Well, when he is trying to solve a technical problem, say for example his takeaway or the position at the top of his backswing, he should think of images too. I'm not saying we don't need coaches, just that the way we think is just as important. Stop using language and gimmicks from golf magazines and start focusing on images. Perhaps think of yourself as Tiger Woods, hitting the ball. That would be a start.

See it in your mind and try to copy it. This way of thinking is in conjunction with a coach, not instead of him. You have a mind for playing and a mind for practise. You have to go to a good coach to improve and you need a mind to help you control certain emotions and thoughts which can help get into these bubbles, to get in the zone. Then you'll play well more often, get your handicap down and take the cash off you pals on a Sunday morning.

As I've said before, Tour players and 18-handicappers have many things in common. They do the same things wrong. Most of their problems come when they are over the ball, and they get distracted, and start thinking of their family, the out-of-bounds fence, the lake, or opening the clubface on the backswing.

Either way they'll get the same results - bad shots. So the 18-handicapper might slice his shot out of bounds or thin his approach but the professional player will miss a green or a putt and end up shooting 73, which isn't much good on the Tour. If he continues to think that way he'll miss the cut, earn no money and lose his card.

They each need a way to access the zone more often so that it isn't just an accident. The best way to do this is to create an image inside your head of exactly what you are trying to do, whether it's holing a putt or hitting a two-iron over a lake to a tight pin 220 yards away. Think about success, see it in you mind, especially over the ball.

You stare at the flag, come back to the ball and see the image of the flag in your mind. It could be a moving image, a video of the flag fluttering in the breeze or it can be a still image, a photograph in your mind. Your brain reacts to what you put into to it. If you put in a bad shot your brain will create a bad shot, if you put in a target, your brain will mobilise all its resources to get that ball to the target.

When you practise you must split your session evenly. One shot should be on whatever technical aspect you are trying to improve. You should follow this with a mental rehearsal of your pre-shot routine, and focus on a picture of the target in your mind. Seeing the target clearly works for EVERY player I have ever worked with. If the target is clear they hit a better shot than if it is fuzzy.

You will achieve this if you work on what psychologists refer to as sub-modalities. I'll explain this in a later chapter. One final thought that will help all players - relive a great shot you have played. That was the mental key Fred Couples used throughout his career.

Jack Nicklaus often said that he 'went to the movies' which meant he saw video footage of the perfect shot in his mind before he actually hit the ball. I know many people find this hard so the next best thing is to visualise a great shot you've actually played yourself and the more detail you give to the memory the more successful you will be. This will give you the buzz and the high that will put you in a bubble. You must bombard your mind with good shots.

You don't have to be a pro to have experienced that. We've all hit dozens of good shots at some time in the past, whatever our level of ability. It could be a drive or a birdie or a hole in one. Anything. Even a 24-handicapper has hit plenty of great shots. That's why he keeps going back.

We all want to get into the zone more often - the main way to do this is imagery. It will take time but when it comes the magic will start. That's what Stephen

Gallacher used to shoot nine-under for 14 holes. It will help you, too.

Update: I'm pleased to report that Stephen is continuing to improve and fulfil his dreams. In 2003 he finished 50th in the Volvo Tour Order of Merit, winning well over £300,000 and finishing in the top ten five times. The following season was sensational. Stephen was spectacularly consistent, winning more than £700,000 to finish 15th on the Order of Merit. He recorded ten top 20 finishes and was ranked in the world's top 50. The finest moment was his first Tour victory when he won the Dunhill Links Championship at St Andrew's, with a four-round total of 19-under-par, defeating Graeme McDowell in a sudden death play-off. Stephen beat a world class field that included Fred Couples, Ernie Els, Vijay Singh, Colin Montgomerie and Retief Goosen. Stephen is one of the most talented players I have ever worked with..

CHAPTER TWELVE

Course Management

Dean

As your golf improves, you will pick up what is known as 'tacit knowledge'. This is what you learn as you experience different situations – in short, you learn from making mistakes. So most of us have already gained a substantial knowledge of course management from the situations we have found ourselves and, of course, how we dealt with them.

I've already told you about a classic case of bad course management that probably cost me a European Tour win and a lot of money. I'm talking about my attempt to win the PGA Championship at Wentworth in 1998 when I was up against Colin Montgomerie.

I was under the severest pressure and that caused a bad mistake in my course management. I was uncontrollably nervous and I decided to hit a three wood on the tight 16th - you may remember I went on to double bogey the hole after hitting and tee shot into the bushes. Looking back, I know now I should have taken a two or three iron to get the ball in play and on the fairway. That sort of thinking is comparable to an experienced professional boxer holding onto the ropes to gain a breather, compared with a young fighter who'll come out searching for a big hit and end up out for the count.

Let's start by taking a look at how professional golfers use practice rounds. All we are interested in is gathering information that will enable us to play the course in the least number of shots. This knowledge can change dramatically depending on the weather and course conditions. You have to allow for that.

So all pros produce a game plan for every hole. We work everything out scientifically based on lengths of the tee, bunkers and out-of-bounds. So we have a strategy for every hole in the same way a general might plan a military campaign. Every shot and every eventuality is accounted for. We calculate risk and reward. We work out, for example, if hitting a driver on a short but tight par four is a worthwhile option.

Course management is all about using your shots wisely. The goal is to play to, or below, your handicap, yet most club golfers, when they get on the course in a medal competition, have not figured out a sensible game plan that takes into consideration what their handicap is.

Their aim is to par every hole when we all know that's not going to happen. That's tough for a pro, never mind a 24 handicapper. So be clear what you goals are, and how realistic they are to the competition you are in. It's different for strokeplay and matchplay play too.

Take the tenth hole at The Belfry. It's one of the most famous holes in golf because of its dramatic links with the Ryder Cup. You are faced with a long open fairway, and a narrow green to the right, surrounded by water and tall trees. The hole is a very short par four, less than 300 yards, and you have a variety of options available to you.

You can lay up with a seven iron off the tee, leaving the full length of the green to aim for. Or you could take a longer club, say a four iron, and have a shorter second but the downside is you'll be playing to the narrowest part of the green. Finally, of course, you can try to drive the green, which is without doubt, high risk for the ultimate reward - a two-putt birdie or even a chance of an eagle two. But beware, you could end up with an eight, or worse, and ruin your round.

Remember the majority of pros in the 2002 Ryder Cup laid up so if they thought the risk wasn't worth taking, it's unlikely that's the shot for you. If you ever play the 10th at The Belfry check where you are on the tee because if you're off the front of the forward yellow tee and the carry is only 240 yards the risk is substantially reduced. In a big tournament, though, you will be off the whites and that 30 or 40 yards will make a huge difference

Remember to weigh up sensibly your chances of success and how likely it is that you can cut a driver 280 yards, through the trees and over the water to a target narrower than your living room. Even Tiger Woods played short in 2002 so ask yourself: Am I letting my heart rule my head?

Let's look at a classic test that you will face on just about every golf course in the world - the long, tough par five. How often do you blast away with your driver and then, if you are lucky enough to hit a decent tee shot, hit a three-wood trying to get as close to the green as possible? Pros don't think like that. Why not take a three wood off the tee, or even a three iron, whatever your favourite club is? Then play short of the green and leave yourself a full shot for your third. Playing sensibly like this, I guarantee that you'll par the hole more times than if you just hit your biggest club, without thinking. And even if you miss the green you'll probably still get a bogey and more often than not, you'll be receiving a shot anyway.

The one thing I can't emphasise enough is 'know your abilities.' Use your shots. And know when a bogey is a good score. If you hit a tee shot into a pot bunker, for example, the rule is, get out first time. Don't be greedy and try to hit a long iron - take your medicine, get the ball back onto the fairway and take it from there. The same applies to trees or bad lies in the rough.

If you take too much club out of a tough bunker, you run a high risk of leaving the ball in the sand and wasting a shot. If you salvage a bogey from a bunker you will have done well so it is not necessary to be overly aggressive. Golf is all about keeping big numbers off your scorecard - especially in stroke play.

Another tip that seems obvious is never give up. I see players becoming discouraged after one bad shot or an unlucky bounce every time I play in Pro-Ams. Stay committed to your process and routine. Don't lose concentration and follow Dr. John's teaching by putting all those negative thoughts out of your mind.

We have a phrase on Tour I'm sure you'll all be familiar with - sucker pins. They are what they say. And the trick is to keep away from them. Modern day professionals are so skilled that the only way tournament organisers have of stopping top players from demolishing their courses and shooting ridiculously low scores is to tuck the pins behind bunkers and small knolls on the greens – anything to make them inaccessible.

Often, top players will choose different targets from the pin. No one can birdie every hole on the course. Most of the time professionals will aim away from the hole and into the fat part of the green. The key word you hear all the pros saying over and over again is patience. We tell ourselves that all the time. There will be sucker pins on courses you play too. So watch out for them and play away from trouble.

It's imperative to be patient and that will go a long way to making you more consistent. Mind you, some pros aren't like that.

Take Phil Mickelson. He makes a massive amount of birdies and eagles, probably more than any other player on the US Tour, but he also throws in a stack of bogeys and even double bogeys. His game plan is just to fire at the pins all the time. Phil is an awesome player yet he still hasn't won a Major. Most people think that's because he's too aggressive. He chooses to entertain and that's the only way Phil knows how to play. He's a very exciting player but I'm sure he would have won a Major by now if he had not been so aggressive with those sucker pins.

The Rules of Golf are complicated but knowing your options can help you. If you spend the odd hour reading through them it will repay you many times over in your golfing life. For example there are many circumstances that you can gain relief without penalty, say, from immovable obstructions or if you are standing on a drain or a sprinkler head.

How about unplayable lies? I'll bet the majority of amateurs don't know exactly what their options are. So what can you do if your ball is at the bottom of a bush or in thick rough? You have four choices. Firstly, you can go back to where you played your last shot and add one. So if you hit your tee shot off line you would be playing three off the tee. Secondly you can go back as far as you want, keeping the pin and the ball in a straight line for a one shot penalty. Thirdly you can have a go and play it. And finally you can take an unplayable lie, which means dropping the ball, not nearer the hole within two club lengths. A lot of players don't realise that when you drop the ball within two club lengths it can roll another two club lengths and the ball is still in play. So the rules can help you if you know how to use them to your advantage.

Another saying pros use all the time is fairways and greens. Golf is not about how far you hit the ball but the number on your scorecard. A professional might only use his driver a couple of times in a round. In fact, it's not uncommon for Tour players to leave their drivers in the locker room on a particularly tight course. You can learn from that. Analyse the hole and calculate where a decent drive might go and if you're bringing bunkers into play. Remember, you can be too near a green. Tour professionals have an optimum distance where they prefer to pitch from, say 80 yards, which might be a smooth sand iron for a particular player. He would rather be 80 yards away from the pin than, say, 65 yards. That distance is not random. He'll have worked this out on the practise ground. You can do that too. It's easy. Find your ideal pitching length and then work backwards from the green to leave the ball around your favourite distance. You'll feel confident, especially if you have played this shot hundreds of times in practice.

We've already talked generally about matchplay and strokeplay tournaments. There is a slightly different approach required for each one. It's pretty obvious that the worst thing that can happen to you in matchplay is loss of hole, whereas in strokeplay a big number, say a nine or ten, would probably ruin your score. So in matchplay you can take risks and be more aggressive but there's one vital tip I have. Always make your opponent win the hole - don't give it to him. Don't be like Kevin Costner in the movie *Tin Cup* when he hit one shot after another into the trees or the water. If you're in trouble, get your ball back in play and on the green - who knows, you might hole a long putt, but even if you don't, make your opponent work.

Most amateur strokeplay events are over 18 holes but it's that word patience again that should be your key thought. It's a marathon, not a sprint. Start off steady, if you have plenty of shots there's nothing wrong with a bogey on the first. Take it and use your shots wisely. Play conservatively, aim for the big part of the greens, away from the bunkers and try not to three-putt.

Finally, like all the Tour pros, I have played in hundreds of Pro-Ams and I've learnt so much about common mistakes that high handicap amateurs make. But the single, most important piece of advice I can give you is to slow down. Just about every time I play with amateurs they try to hit the ball too hard and keep up with me, obviously that means they hit driver all the time and we've already talked about how destructive that can be. Amateurs should learn relaxation techniques that will calm them down and control their nerves and excitement. And they should focus on a smooth and even tempo, play within themselves and to their strengths.

Playing golf outside the Tour should be a leisure activity, mostly conducted in beautiful surroundings. If you hit a bad shot take a tip off Tiger Woods and look at the next shot as a challenge. Think sensibly and you can come off the course contented and with your goals fulfilled. Remember, above all, golf should be about fun. So go out and enjoy yourself.

A Biography

Dr. John

Dr. John Pates was born on January 30, 1966, in the heart of Birmingham. He spent the first eight months of his life in a foster home before he was adopted by Ken and Nancy Pates. Dr. John grew up in Northfield, south Birmingham, a working-class community where the majority of the population relied on the Longbridge car plant for employment. Ken was a printer and Nancy contributed to the family finances through her work as a skilled seamstress, making quality dresses for a wealthy clientele.

Dr. John was a multi-talented sportsman as a young schoolboy, excelling in cricket, as a reliable all-rounder, basketball and soccer, as an athletic goalkeeper. He represented his district at all three sports throughout his school career.

Dr. John attended Shenley Court Comprehensive School - the largest school in the Midlands - breezing through his GCE O Levels, excelling in Biology, Chemistry, English and Physics, before earning a B-Tech Diploma for Sciences at Birmingham's Matthew Bolton College.

He considered a career in veterinary science but turned his back on the animal world to pursue more academic qualifications at Bangor University where he acquired a 2:1 degree in Physical Education and Psychology. Dr. John stayed on an extra year to pick up another qualification in statistics, gaining knowledge that would prove invaluable in later years when he sought to make sense of the role of the mind in sporting excellence.

The following year, Dr. John gained more experience in a university in Nova Scotia, Canada, before returning to the United Kingdom to continue accumulating qualifications at Brighton University where he earned a Post Graduate Certificate of Education which enabled him to teach Physical Education anywhere in the country. He specialised in teaching special needs students.

At the age of 22, Dr. John returned to Birmingham to teach PE at Bartley Green Comprehensive School but, after a year, he returned to Bangor to earn a Masters of Philosophy in Sports Psychology. Dr. John continued to play a range of sports but he was particularly successful at basketball, playing in the National League for Stevenage, Greenwich and Worthing as a forward/shooting guard. He captained and coached his university side at Bangor, helping the team from the smallest university in Great Britain to qualify for two national finals. Dr. John also represented Welsh Universities but he was still driven by the need to broaden his scientific knowledge, earning further qualifications in hypnosis and Neuro Linguistic Programming, a revolutionary system of positive thinking that is used by many professional golfers today.

Dr. John returned to the classroom at Havering Sixth Form College, Hornchurch, where he taught PE and A Level Psychology. His growing reputation had earned him a scholarship with The Full Bright Programme, which enabled him to teach Pure Psychology in a community college in Laredo, Texas. When he was in the States, Dr. John picked up a persistent ankle injury playing basketball. He could not shake off the problem and turned to golf for athletic fulfilment.

After returning to the UK, Dr. John took up a post at Sheffield's Hallam University, continuing to broaden his knowledge by completing a PhD on the effects of hypnosis on peak performance states in professional basketball players and golfers. It was in Sheffield that Dr. John began developing his unique teaching methods designed to help sportsmen and women use the power of their minds to control emotions, feelings and thoughts associated with the zone.

He joined Beauchef Golf Club in Sheffield, reducing his handicap from 20 to five, in less than three years, despite rarely practising and infrequent playing. Dr. John now began working with various sportsmen and women in the Midlands, enjoying considerable success and earning a growing reputation for his revolutionary methods. Yorkshire Tour player Robert Wragg was the first professional golfer to benefit from Dr. John's teaching. He was quickly followed by basketball players, world champion racing car drivers, hockey stars and other fringe Tour players, many of whom employed Peter Cowan as their coach. Through Peter, Dr. John met Darren Clarke, one of the world's greatest players.

Darren was frustrated and dispirited after shooting 84 in the Pro-Am preceding the 2002 English Open at the Forest of Arden. The Irishman was in a slump. He had only recorded two top 10 finishes that season and Darren was becoming bewildered by his inability to find a solution. The details of their meeting are described in another chapter but Dr. John spent three hours with Darren the night before the first round, transforming his mental skills. The following day the Irishman carded 65 and went on to win the tournament with a final total of 17-under-par – three ahead of Soren Hansen from Denmark.

Darren's incredible transformation was primarily due to Dr. John's teaching. The Irishman was so impressed that he wanted his help permanently. Three days later, Dr. John was in an aeroplane heading for New York and Bethpage State Park, where the 2002 US Open was being played. It was a fairytale accomplishment for Dr. John as he watching the opening two rounds when Darren played with Chris Dimarco and Tiger Woods, who went on to win the championship, three ahead of Phil Mickelson. Darren continued his good form, finished in the top 25.

Back on the European Tour, Dr. John's reputation was spreading. New players sought his help, including 2006 Ryder Cup captain, former worlds number one and 1991 Masters champion Ian Woosnam. Other notable players Dr. John has assisted include Thomas Bjorn (Ryder Cup Star and Winner of 14 tour events), Graham Mcdowel (2008 Ryder cup player and winner of the 2008 Barclays Scottish Open), Steve Gallacher (Winner of the 2004 Dunhill Championships) Jean Van De Velde (Ryder Cup Star and winner of the 2006 Madiera Open), Bradley Dredge (Winner of the 2005 World Cup and 2006 Swiss Open), Steve Webster (Winner of the 2007 Portugual Masters), Gary Orr (Winner of three European Tour events) and many others. Taken together Dr. John has coached over 15 European tour champions.

Dr. John began working with forty-year-old Tour veteran Paul Broadhurst in 2003. Paul, who turned professional in 1989, began his career successfully and with great consistency. He was only once out of the European Tour Order of Merit

Top 50 in his first 11 years. His CV up to that point made impressive reading - six tournament wins, a record-equalling 63 in the Open Championship at St Andrew's in 1990 and a 100 per cent record in the 1991 Ryder Cup match at Kiawah Island, when he defeated Mark O'Meara in the singles and joined Ian Woosnam to beat Paul Azinger and Hale Irwin in the doubles. Then he suffered a career-threatening wrist injury in 2000. He only played in six tournaments, winning just £25,000. The following year, Paul missed 16 cuts and lost his card after finishing 157th in the Order of Merit. In 2002 he was still struggling, missing 11 cuts and languishing 141st in the Order of Merit. He won barely £100,000 in three years. His career was transformed when he began working with Dr. John Pates at the 2003 South African Open. Paul went on the make 15 cuts, earn £150,000 and finish 89th on the Order of Merit.

In 2004, Paul missed just nine cuts, finished 44th and winning more than £320,000 in prize money. In the 2005 season, Paul finished in the top 30 of the Order of Merit with more than £600,000 in prize money. In April, he won his first tournament for more than 10 years when he lifted the Portuguese Open at Quinta da Marinha with a four-round total of 13-under-par to land a winner's cheque of £140,000. He finished that year ranked in the world's top 50. In 2006 he won the Portuguese Open again and missed out on the Ryder Cup squad by one place.

In 2005 Dr. John began working with Bradley Dredge, who was a talented player not quite living up to his potential. He turned professional in 1996 and had won just one tournament in eight years - the 2003 Madeira Open. The following year was another disappointing season - no wins, a 60th finish in the Order of Merit, six missed cuts and just two top 10s.

Bradley worked hard in the winter of 2005 but he performed moderately in the first six tournaments, missing two cuts and shooting an 83 in the Spanish Open. Then he met Dr. John and the change in his mind and his scores was dramatic and immediate.

Bradley worked with Dr. John for just two days before heading for the Italian Open, hitting the ball well and sensing a fundamental change in his mind on the golf course. He finished second behind Steve Webster, with a 15-under-par total of 273. In the next 14 tournaments, Bradley missed just one cut, made seven top 10 finishes and amassed more than £1.2 million pounds winning the World Cup of golf at the end of his first season working with Dr. John. The following year Bradley then went on to win the Swiss Open and become a world's top 50 player.

Dr. John plans to continue helping professional golfers across the world and has widened his business interests to include writing coaching courses for the PGA and presenting business and golf psychology workshops.

A Biography

Dean Robertson

Dean Robertson was born on July 11, 1970. He grew up in Paisley on the outskirts of Glasgow where his father David was a huge influence in the early years of his golfing career. David was a scratch golfer for more than 25 years and still plays a mean game today off two-handicap.

David presented Dean with his first set of clubs at the age of five, an old set with cut-down shafts that had once belonged to his grandfather. Dean began accompanying his father at the local club Cochran Castle when he was around five-years-old, going on to join the junior section on his tenth birthday.

He reduced his handicap to five when he was 16 and went on to win his first trophy – the club's junior championship. Dean was small and a short hitter and many doubted his ability to overcome his lack of power.

"I was so small," says Dean. "I was a really late developer. I was tiny. The year I won the junior championship I remember hitting a three-wood to the par three opening hole, which is just 170 yards. Now, more often than not, I can get there with a seven iron."

Dean worked at his game diligently, following the traditional route to representative honours, playing for

Renfrewshire County Boys before advancing into the County Open Age B team and forcing his way into the first team squad at the age of just 17.

He left school and began working as a trainee civil engineer but Dean was determined to make a career out of the game he loved, earning a scholarship to the Midland Junior College at Texas, joining fellow Scot Andrew Coltart.

Dean reduced his handicap to plus one and began his assault on the Scottish amateur scene. He was 19 now and, in a glittering season, played for Scotland Youths and won the Scottish Youth Championship at Hilton Park. The following year, Dean reduced his handicap to plus three, earned his first full Scottish cap and represented Great Britain and Ireland Youths at Dalmahoy.

In 1992, Dean won a host of top Scottish strokeplay events and represented his country in the Home Internationals at Prestwick, going on to play for Great Britain and Ireland in the St Andrews Trophy at Royal Cinque Ports in Kent. He won the Scottish Amateur Strokeplay Championships at Morton Hall, Edinburgh and again represented Great Britain and Ireland in the Eisenhower Trophy along with Bradley Dredge, Raymond Burns and Matthew Stanford.

The following year, his last in the amateur game, Dean won the Scottish Amateur Championships on the historic links at Royal Dornoch, and represented Scotland twice - in the six-man European Championships in the Czech Republic and the Home Internationals at Hoylake.

Dean was now widely regarded as one of the best players in the country and later that year earned the ultimate honour in the amateur game when he represented

Great Britain and Ireland in the Walker Cup at Interlachen Country Club in Minnesota. His team-mates included Padraig Harrington, Bradley Dredge, Raymond Burns, Ian Pyman and Raymond Russell. The Europeans lost badly but Dean played well, defeating the vastly experienced Jay Sigel 3 and 2 in the singles.

Dean spent the following winter labouring on a building site and stacking supermarket shelves, before turning his back on the amateur game and making his first attempt at earning his European Tour card.

After missing out on a Tour place, Dean played the following season on the Tartan Tour under the guidance of Keith Campbell at Gleddoch, Langbank. Dean played well in his first tournament, the Scottish PGA Championship, winning £3,500 for a third-place finish behind champion Andrew Coltart, who defeated Gary Orr in a play-off.

Later that year Dean gained his Tour card on the rain-soaked fairways of Massan in France when he sneaked through in a 14-man play-off for just two spots by chipping in on the first extra hole.

Dean finished fourth in his first tournament at the Madeira Island Open and went on to enjoy an outstanding opening season, finishing just outside the top 50 and earning well over £100,000.

He went on to become a formidable professional golfer, known for his excellent putting, consistently coming in the top ten of the putting statistics on the Tour.

Dean earned more than £116,000 when he won the 1999 Italian Open at Circolo Golf Club in Turin, holding off the challenge of Padraig Harrington. Other career highlights include representing Scotland in the World Cup of Golf in 1999 and 2001.

After almost 10 years on Tour and earning more than £1.3 million, Dean was forced to walk away from the game for 18 months due to ill health. On his return to golf, Dean no longer competes on the Tour but signed off his playing career with a magnificent victory at the 2006 Scottish PGA Championship at Gleneagles where he shot an amazing 10 under par 63 in the third round. Dean's love for the game and his vast knowledge has led him into his new passion - coaching. He is fast becoming one of the UK's leading peak performance golf coaches. Dean heads up coaching and development for the Scottish Junior Golf Tour and has other business interests which include corporate education, golf schools, seminars and presentations. He is writing further books on peak performance coaching, learning and understanding within the game of golf.

A Biography

Mike Gardner

Mike Gardner is the sports Editor of the Cumbrian News.

He has won awards for journalistic excellence including the prestigious Whitbread Feature Writer of the year in 1990. Author of 'Willie' the life and times of Rugby League legend Willie Horne, Mike has enjoyed a fantastic career reporting on the affairs of Barrow RFLC, Carlisle F.C and Sport in the North West of England.

Mike is a good Amateur Golfer and enjoyed a moderate career in Rugby League as a centre threequater with Corporation Combine ARLFC.

He is married to Lesley. They have two sons Dr. John who is a Science teacher and David who is an IT consultant and a County Champion golfer. Mike has been a best friend of Dr. John and Dean for more than 8 years and without his incredible effort and help this book would have not been written.

Lightning Source UK Ltd.
Milton Keynes UK
UKOW051618120712

195897UK00001B/1/P